Taste of Home

Copycat

RESTAURANT
FAVORITES

Copycat
RESTAURANT
FAVORITES

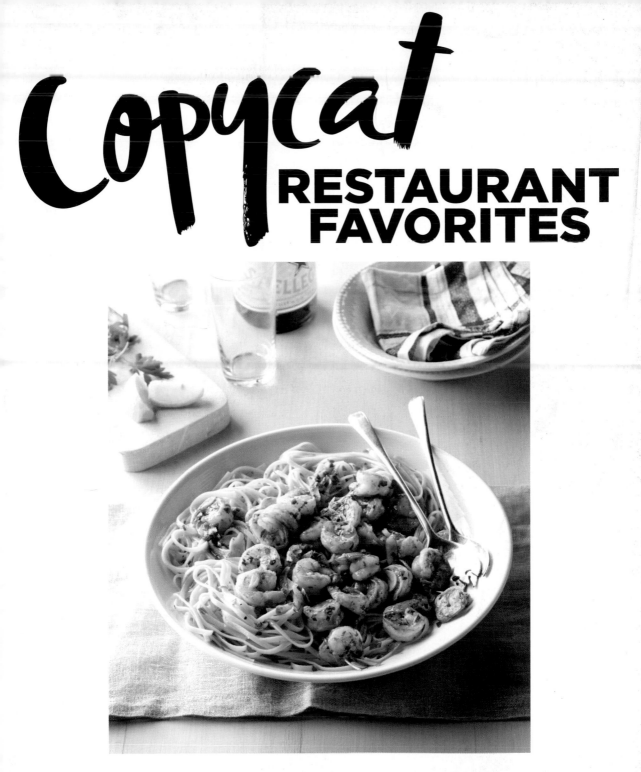

TASTE OF HOME BOOKS • RDA ENTHUSIAST BRANDS, LLC • MILWAUKEE, WI

Taste of Home

© 2020 RDA Enthusiast Brands, LLC.
1610 N. 2nd St., Suite 102, Milwaukee WI 53212-3906
All rights reserved. Taste of Home is a registered trademark of RDA Enthusiast Brands, LLC.
Visit us at *tasteofhome.com* for other Taste of Home books and products.

ISBN: 978-1-61765-860-0
LOCC: 2019945236

Deputy Editor: Mark Hagen
Senior Art Director: Raeann Thompson
Editor: Amy Glander
Art Director: Maggie Conners
Designer: Arielle Jardine
Copy Editor: Ann Walter
Cover Photographer: Grace Natoli Sheldon
Cover Set Stylist: Stephanie Marchese
Cover Food Stylist: Kathryn Conrad

Pictured on front cover:
Cappuccino Cinnamon Rolls, p. 17

Pictured on title page:
Garlic Lemon Shrimp, p. 179

Pictured on back cover:
Bacon Cheddar Potato Skins, p. 69
Peanut Butter Cup Cheesecake, p. 230
Fantastic Fish Tacos, p. 171

Printed in China
10

TABLE OF CONTENTS

Dig in to the flavor and fun of today's most popular restaurant dishes when you cook from the fantastic all-new collection **Taste of Home Copycat Restaurant Favorites.** Want to learn the secrets behind the menu items you crave most? Take a look inside and you'll discover how to whip up those dishes in your own kitchen.

From eye-opening morning staples and savory weeknight dinners to bakeshop specialties and classic desserts, you'll find the perfect recipe here. Save money, skip the drive-thru and enjoy the mouthwatering delights found on today's menus from the comfort of your own home. It's easy with this edition of **Copycat Restaurant Favorites.**

GET SOCIAL WITH US

LIKE US: facebook.com/tasteofhome | **PIN US:** pinterest.com/taste_of_home
FOLLOW US: @tasteofhome | **TWEET US:** twitter.com/tasteofhome

TO FIND A RECIPE:
tasteofhome.com

TO SUBMIT A RECIPE:
tasteofhome.com/submit

TO FIND OUT ABOUT OTHER
***TASTE OF HOME* PRODUCTS:**
shoptasteofhome.com

Prepare Today's Top Restaurant Dishes Yourself

Skip the delivery, avoid the drive-thru and keep that tip money in your wallet, because *Taste of Home Copycat Restaurant Favorites* brings America's most popular menu items to your kitchen. Dive into this incredible collection, and you'll learn the secret ingredients behind the tastiest bites found in the country's most popular coffee shops, restaurants, pizzerias and all of the other hot spots you hit up the most.

Get cooking with hundreds of no-fuss recipes inspired by Starbucks, McDonald's, California Pizza Kitchen, Olive Garden, Panera Bread, Cinnabon, The Cheesecake Factory, Applebee's, TGI Fridays, Cracker Barrel and so many others.

TAKE A LOOK AT SOME OF THE BITES YOU'LL FIND INSIDE

EYE-OPENING BREAKFASTS
Why get up early to beat the morning breakfast crowd? Instead, savor pancakes, cinnamon rolls, burritos and other morning delights at home. Bonus: You can cook in your slippers and pj's.

COFFEE SHOP FAVORITES
Save money when you brew your own specialty beverages at home. You'll also find doughnuts, muffins and all of the dunk-able nibbles that make coffee-shop stops so sweet.

BEST APPETIZERS EVER
It's time to nosh on deep-fried mac and cheese, Asian pot stickers, baked pretzels, jalapeno poppers and fried pickles—all from the comfort of home! Call the gang over, because this is finger-food overload!

COPYCAT ENTREES
Settle in for the out-to-eat greats you enjoy most—without getting in the car! Try everything from juicy burgers and ribs slathered in sauce to mouthwatering salmon and tender roast beef with the gravy you can't enough of.

P. 33

P. 236

P. 184

POPULAR PIZZA & PASTA

You don't have to wait on the delivery guy to chow down on your favorite pizza. Simply turn to this incredible chapter and re-create your family's favorite "za" in your own kitchen. You'll also find pastas that will make you feel as if you're in your favorite Italian eatery.

DOUBLE-TAKE DESSERTS

Skip the bakery and ice cream parlor when you whip up these after-dinner specialties. Perfect for cozy nights in or meals with weekend guests, these delectable copycat treats make every occasion a bit sweeter.

You can prepare these restaurant staples with confidence, knowing that every dish was tested and approved at the *Taste of Home* Test Kitchen. No matter which dishes you whip up, they're sure to turn out perfect every time. In addition, each recipe offers a complete set of nutrition facts, so you know exactly what you're serving.

So dig in to the savory (and sweet) menu classics that you crave most today—all from the comfort of your own home. **With *Taste of Home Copycat Restaurant Favorites* it's never been faster, more convenient or tastier!**

Eye-Opening Breakfasts

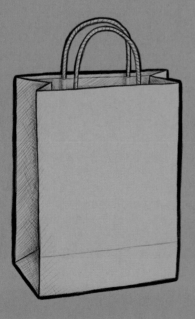

YOU LOVE YOUR LOCAL PANCAKE HOUSE AND DOUGHNUT SHOP, BUT NOW YOU CAN SKIP THE WAIT, THE BILL AND THE TIP BY MAKING YOUR OWN BREAKFAST CREATIONS AT HOME. THESE DELICIOUS RIFFS ON RESTAURANT FAVES WILL START YOUR DAY OFF RIGHT!

COFFEE-GLAZED DOUGHNUTS, P. 29
INSPIRED BY: DUNKIN' DONUTS'
GLAZED DONUT

BERRY-TOPPED COFFEE CAKE

This lovely coffee cake is loaded with fresh berries. It's perfect for anyone with a sweet tooth. Serve with hot coffee or tea.
—Heather O'Neill, Troy, OH

PREP: 25 min. • **BAKE:** 45 min. + cooling • **MAKES:** 10 servings

- ⅓ cup butter, softened
- ⅔ cup sugar
- 1 large egg, room temperature
- 2 tsp. grated lemon zest
- ¾ cup all-purpose flour
- ¾ cup whole wheat flour
- ½ tsp. baking powder
- ¼ tsp. salt
- ¼ tsp. baking soda
- ½ cup reduced-fat sour cream

TOPPING
- ⅓ cup sugar
- 2 tsp. all-purpose flour
- ½ tsp. ground cinnamon
- 1 cup fresh or frozen blueberries, thawed
- ½ cup fresh or frozen unsweetened raspberries, thawed

GLAZE
- ⅓ cup confectioners' sugar
- 2 tsp. fat-free milk
- ⅛ tsp. vanilla extract

1. Preheat the oven to 350°. Grease a 9-in. springform pan.
2. Cream butter and sugar until light and fluffy. Beat in egg and lemon zest. In another bowl, whisk together flours, baking powder, salt and baking soda; add to creamed mixture alternately with sour cream, beating well (batter will be thick). Spread into prepared springform pan.
3. For topping, mix sugar, flour and cinnamon; toss gently with berries. Distribute over batter to within 1 in. of sides. Bake until a toothpick inserted in center comes out clean, 45-50 minutes. Cool on a wire rack 10 minutes. Remove rim from pan.
4. Mix glaze ingredients. Drizzle over warm coffee cake.

1 SLICE: 246 cal., 8g fat (5g sat. fat), 36mg chol., 180mg sod., 42g carb. (27g sugars, 2g fiber), 4g pro.

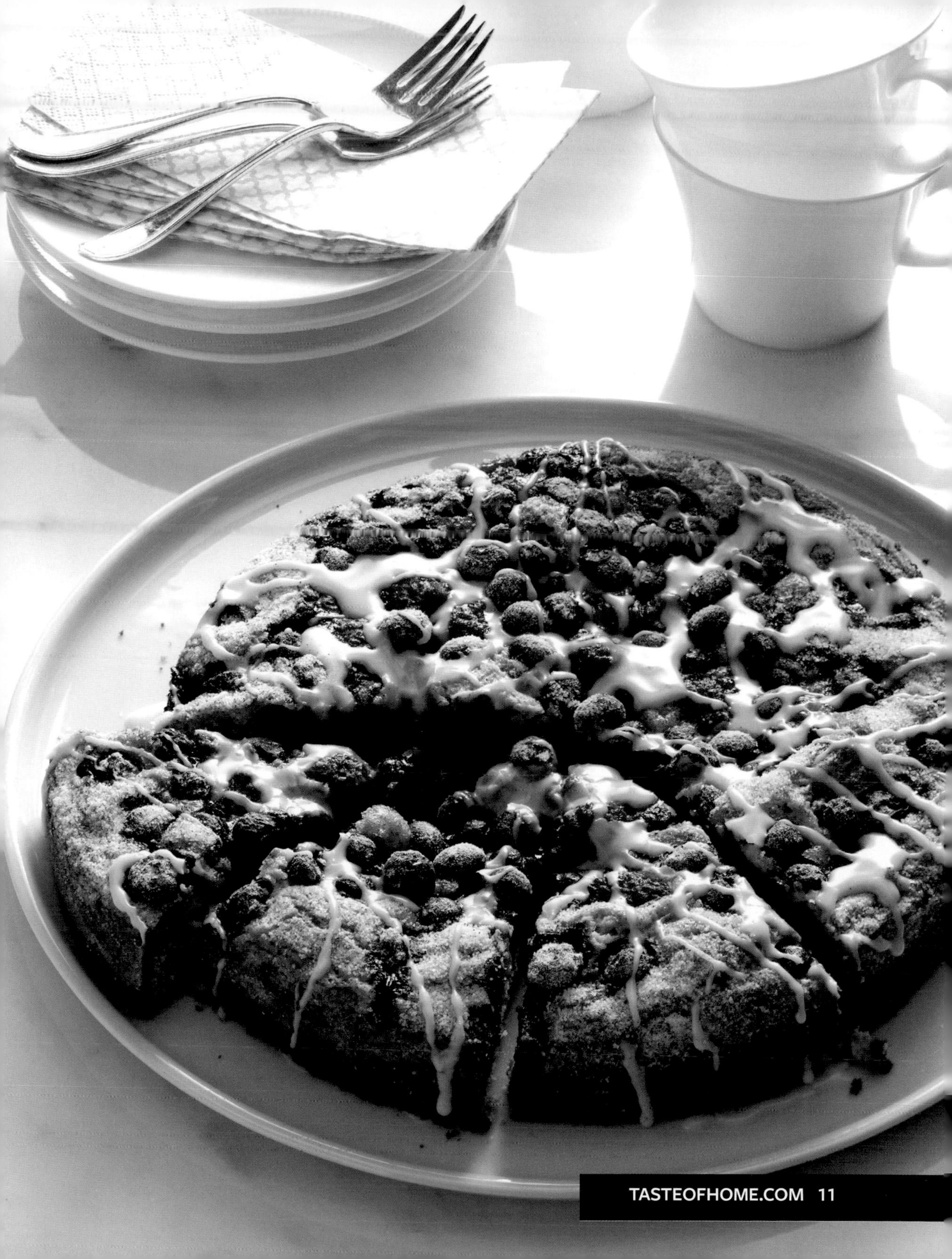

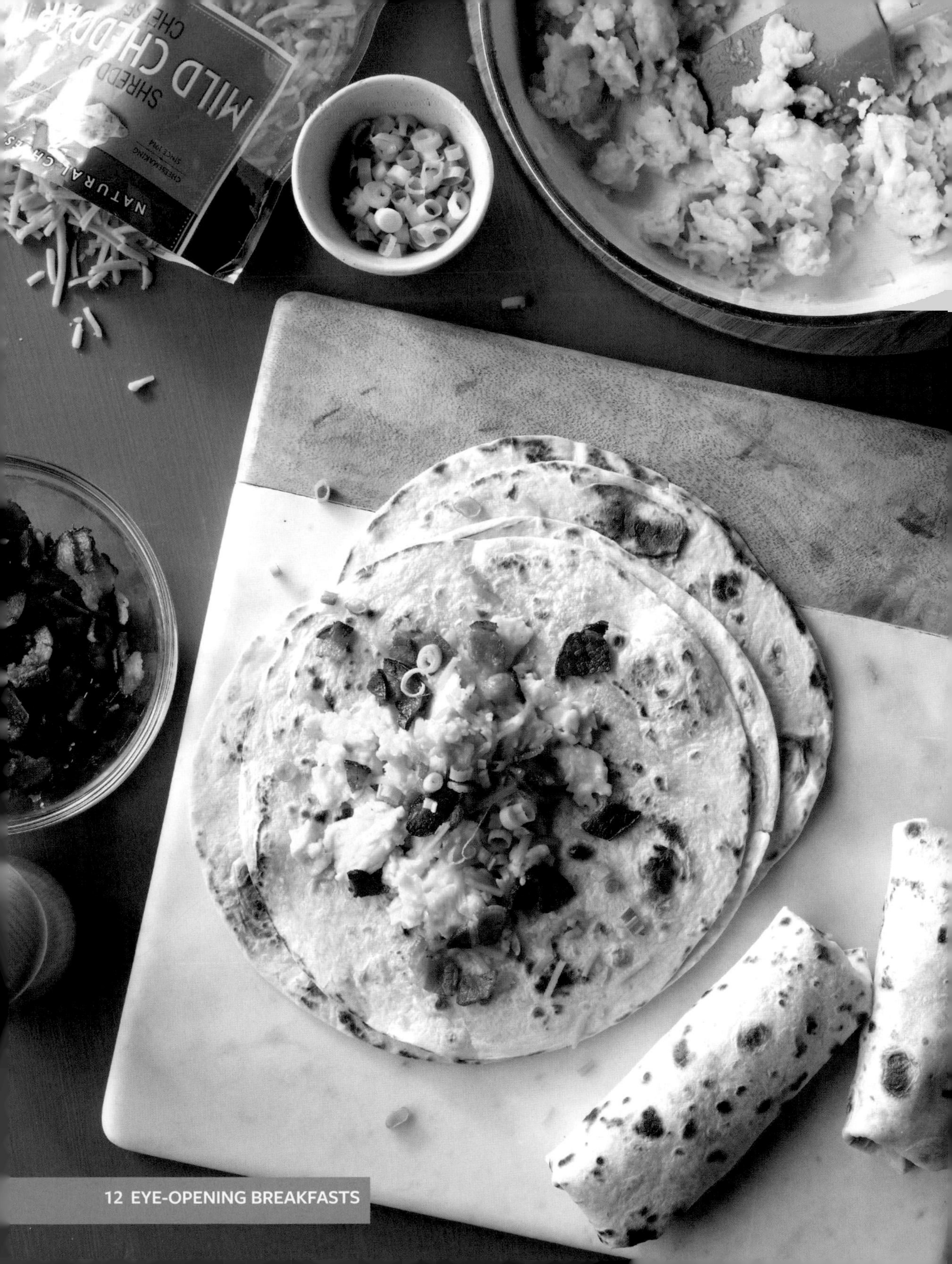

EGG BURRITOS

When I start my day with a real breakfast, I stave off hunger all morning. You can, too, with these easy burritos. Make a batch on a day you have extra time and store them in the freezer. Then zap one in the microwave before you leave the house.
—Audra Niederman, Aberdeen, SD

TAKES: 25 min. • **MAKES:** 10 burritos

- 12 bacon strips, chopped
- 12 large eggs
- ½ tsp. salt
- ¼ tsp. pepper
- 10 flour tortillas (8 in.), warmed
- 1½ cups shredded cheddar cheese
- 4 green onions, thinly sliced

1. In a large cast-iron or other heavy skillet, cook bacon until crisp; drain on paper towels. Remove all but 1-2 Tbsp. drippings from the pan.
2. Whisk together eggs, salt and pepper. Heat skillet over medium heat; pour in egg mixture. Cook and stir until eggs are thickened and no liquid egg remains; remove from heat.
3. Spoon about ¼ cup egg mixture onto center of each tortilla; sprinkle with cheese, bacon and green onions. Roll into burritos.

FREEZE OPTION: Cool eggs before making burritos. Individually wrap the burritos in paper towels and foil; freeze in an airtight container. To use, remove foil; place paper towel-wrapped burrito on a microwave-safe plate. Microwave on high until heated through, turning once. Let stand 15 seconds.

1 BURRITO: 376 cal., 20g fat (8g sat. fat), 251mg chol., 726mg sod., 29g carb. (0 sugars, 2g fiber), 19g pro.

INSPIRED BY;
TACO BELL'S
GRILLED BREAKFAST BURRITO

DAD'S BLUEBERRY BUTTERMILK PANCAKES

My dad makes blueberry pancakes every Saturday. The combination of oats, cornmeal and buttermilk in the batter gives the pancakes a heartiness we can't resist.
—Gabrielle Short, Pleasant Hill, IA

PREP: 15 min. + standing • **COOK:** 10 min./batch
MAKES: 12 pancakes

- 1 cup all-purpose flour
- 3 Tbsp. cornmeal
- 3 Tbsp. quick-cooking oats
- 3 Tbsp. sugar
- 1 tsp. baking powder
- ½ tsp. baking soda
- ½ tsp. salt
  Dash ground nutmeg
- 1 large egg
- 1½ cups buttermilk
- 2 Tbsp. canola oil
- 1 tsp. vanilla extract
- 1 cup fresh or frozen blueberries

1. In a large bowl, whisk the first 8 ingredients. In another bowl, whisk egg, buttermilk, oil and vanilla until blended. Add to flour mixture; stir just until moistened (batter will be lumpy). Let stand 15 minutes.

2. Lightly grease a griddle or large nonstick skillet; heat over medium heat. Stir blueberries into batter. Pour pancake batter by ¼ cupfuls onto griddle or skillet. Cook until bubbles on top begin to pop and bottoms are golden brown. Turn; cook until second side is brown.

3 PANCAKES: 332 cal., 10g fat (2g sat. fat), 50mg chol., 746mg sod., 52g carb. (18g sugars, 2g fiber), 9g pro.

CAPPUCCINO CINNAMON ROLLS

Coffee flavor accents the filling of these ooey-gooey rolls.
—Sherri Cox, Lucasville, OH

PREP: 45 min. + rising • **BAKE:** 25 min. • **MAKES:** 1 dozen

- 1 pkg. (¼ oz.) active dry yeast
- 1 cup warm water (110° to 115°)
- ¾ cup warm whole milk (110° to 115°)
- ½ cup warm buttermilk (110° to 115°)
- 3 Tbsp. sugar
- 2 Tbsp. butter, softened
- 1¼ tsp. salt
- 5½ to 6 cups all-purpose flour

FILLING
- ¼ cup butter, melted
- 1 cup packed brown sugar
- 4 tsp. instant coffee granules
- 2 tsp. ground cinnamon

ICING
- 1½ cups confectioners' sugar
- 2 Tbsp. butter, softened
- 1 to 2 Tbsp. whole milk
- 2 tsp. instant cappuccino mix, optional
- ½ tsp. vanilla extract

1. In a large bowl, dissolve yeast in warm water. Add warm milk, buttermilk, sugar, butter, salt and 4 cups flour. Beat on medium speed until smooth. Stir in enough remaining flour to form a soft dough (dough will be sticky).
2. Turn onto a floured surface; knead until smooth and elastic, 6-8 minutes. Place in a greased bowl, turning once to grease top. Cover and let rise in a warm place until doubled, 1 hour.
3. Punch dough down; turn onto a floured surface. Roll into an 18x12-in. rectangle; brush with butter. Combine brown sugar, coffee granules and cinnamon; sprinkle over dough to within ½ in. of edges.
4. Roll up jelly-roll style, starting with a long side; pinch seam to seal. Cut into 12 slices. Place rolls, cut side down, in a greased 13x9-in. baking pan. Cover and let rise until doubled, 30 minutes.
5. Preheat oven to 350°. Bake 22-28 minutes or until golden brown. Place pan on a wire rack. In a small bowl, beat icing ingredients until smooth. Spread over rolls. Serve warm.
1 ROLL: 436 cal., 9g fat (5g sat. fat), 22mg chol., 328mg sod., 82g carb. (38g sugars, 2g fiber), 7g pro.

GINGERBREAD COFFEE CAKE

At our house, we love gingerbread that's not too sweet. If you prefer it sweeter, drizzle a simple glaze on top. Add chopped crystallized ginger for a pleasant zing.
—Barbara Humiston, Tampa, FL

PREP: 20 min. • **BAKE:** 20 min. + cooling • **MAKES:** 8 servings

- 1 cup all-purpose flour
- ½ cup plus 1 Tbsp. sugar, divided
- 1¾ tsp. ground cinnamon, divided
- 1 tsp. ground ginger
- ¼ tsp. salt
- ¼ tsp. ground allspice
- ¼ cup cold butter
- ¾ tsp. baking powder
- ½ tsp. baking soda
- 1 large egg, room temperature
- ½ cup buttermilk
- 2 Tbsp. molasses

1. Preheat oven to 350°. In a large bowl, mix the flour, ½ cup sugar, ¾ tsp. cinnamon, ginger, salt and allspice; cut in butter until crumbly. Reserve ⅓ cup for topping.

2. Stir baking powder and baking soda into remaining flour mixture. In a small bowl, whisk egg, buttermilk and molasses. Add to flour mixture; stir just until moistened. Transfer batter to a greased 8-in. round baking pan.

3. Add remaining sugar and cinnamon to reserved topping; sprinkle over batter. Bake 20-25 minutes or until a toothpick inserted in center comes out clean. Cool completely in pan on a wire rack.

CONFECTIONERS' SUGAR ICING (OPTIONAL): Mix ¾ cup confectioners' sugar, 1 Tbsp. 2% milk and ½ tsp. vanilla extract. Drizzle over cooled coffee cake. Sprinkle with 2 Tbsp. finely chopped crystallized ginger.

1 SLICE: 195 cal., 7g fat (4g sat. fat), 39mg chol., 283mg sod., 31g carb. (19g sugars, 1g fiber), 3g pro.

DIABETIC EXCHANGES: 2 starch, 1½ fat.

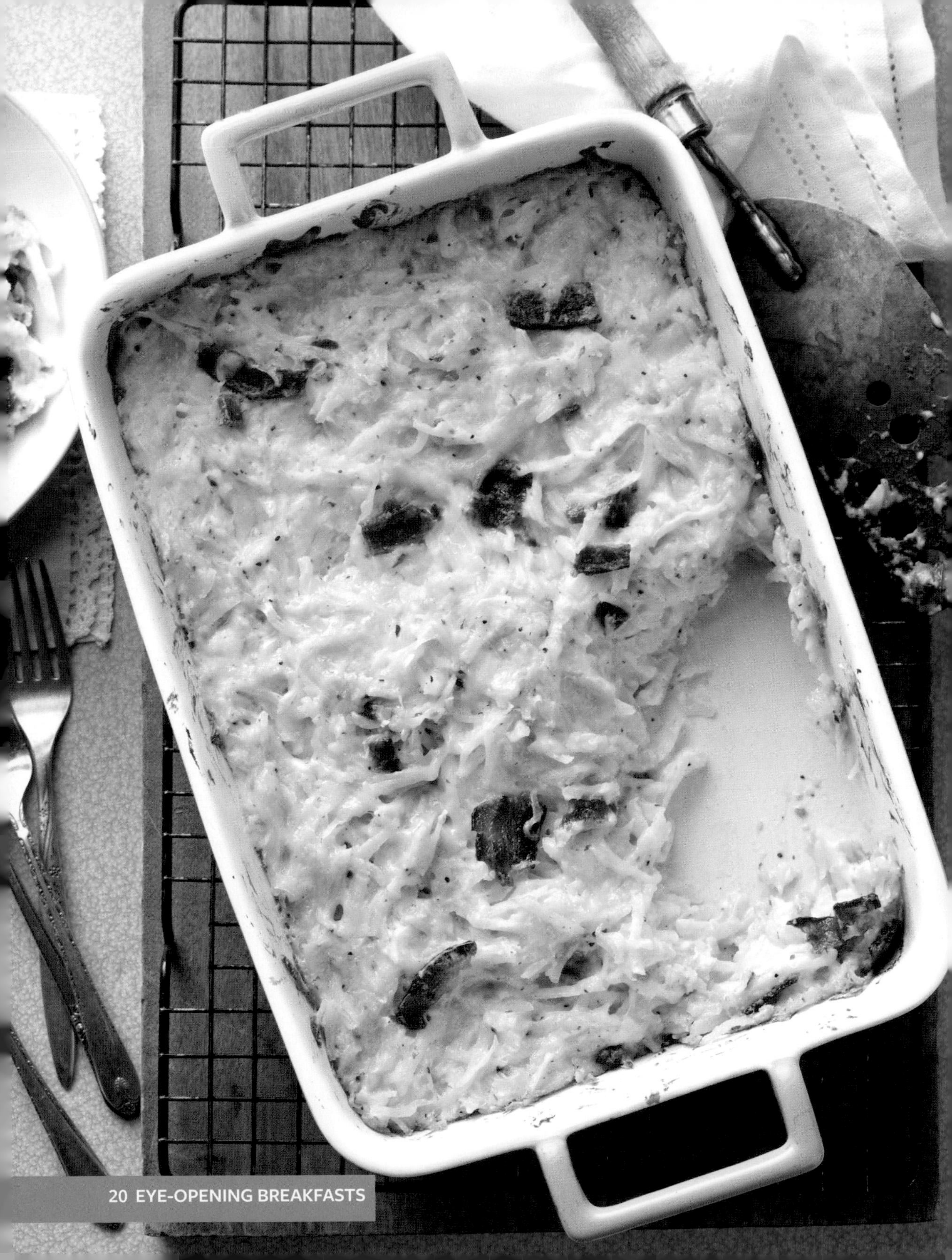

DELUXE HASH BROWN CASSEROLE

My son-in-law gave me the recipe for this casserole, which my kids say is addictive. It's also an amazing make-ahead dish.
—Amy Oswalt, Burr, NE

PREP: 10 min. • **BAKE:** 50 min. • **MAKES:** 12 servings

- 1½ cups sour cream onion dip
- 1 can (10¾ oz.) condensed cream of chicken soup, undiluted
- 1 envelope ranch salad dressing mix
- 1 tsp. onion powder
- 1 tsp. garlic powder
- ½ tsp. pepper
- 1 pkg. (30 oz.) frozen shredded hash brown potatoes, thawed
- 2 cups shredded cheddar cheese
- ½ cup crumbled cooked bacon

Preheat oven to 375°. In a large bowl, mix the first 6 ingredients; stir in potatoes, cheese and bacon. Transfer to a greased 13x9-in. baking dish. Bake until golden brown, 50-60 minutes.

FREEZE OPTION: Cover and freeze unbaked casserole. To use, partially thaw in refrigerator overnight. Remove from refrigerator 30 minutes before baking. Preheat oven to 375°. Bake casserole as directed until top is golden brown and a thermometer inserted in center reads 165°, increasing time to 1¼-1½ hours.

⅔ CUP: 273 cal., 17g fat (6g sat. fat), 36mg chol., 838mg sod., 20g carb. (2g sugars, 2g fiber), 10g pro.

TEX-MEX QUICHE

I discovered this recipe many years ago, and it's still one of my favorites. It's quick, easy and tasty. It's also a good dish to take to potlucks or to serve as an appetizer. You might enjoy it for brunch or a light supper, too.

—Hazel Turner, Houston, TX

PREP: 10 min. • **BAKE:** 45 min. + cooling • **MAKES:** 6 servings

- 1 tsp. chili powder
- 1 pastry shell (9 in.), unbaked
- 1 cup shredded cheddar cheese
- 1 cup shredded Monterey Jack cheese
- 1 Tbsp. all-purpose flour
- 3 large eggs, beaten
- 1½ cups half-and-half cream
- 1 can (4 oz.) chopped green chiles, well drained
- 1 can (2¼ oz.) sliced ripe olives, drained
- 1 tsp. salt
- ¼ tsp. pepper

1. Sprinkle chili powder over the inside of the crust. Combine cheeses with flour and place in crust.
2. Combine eggs, cream, chiles, olives, salt and pepper. Pour over the cheese.
3. Bake at 325° for 45-55 minutes or until a knife inserted in the center comes out clean. Cool for 10 minutes before cutting the quiche into wedges.

1 PIECE: 438 cal., 30g fat (17g sat. fat), 180mg chol., 985mg sod., 23g carb. (4g sugars, 1g fiber), 15g pro.

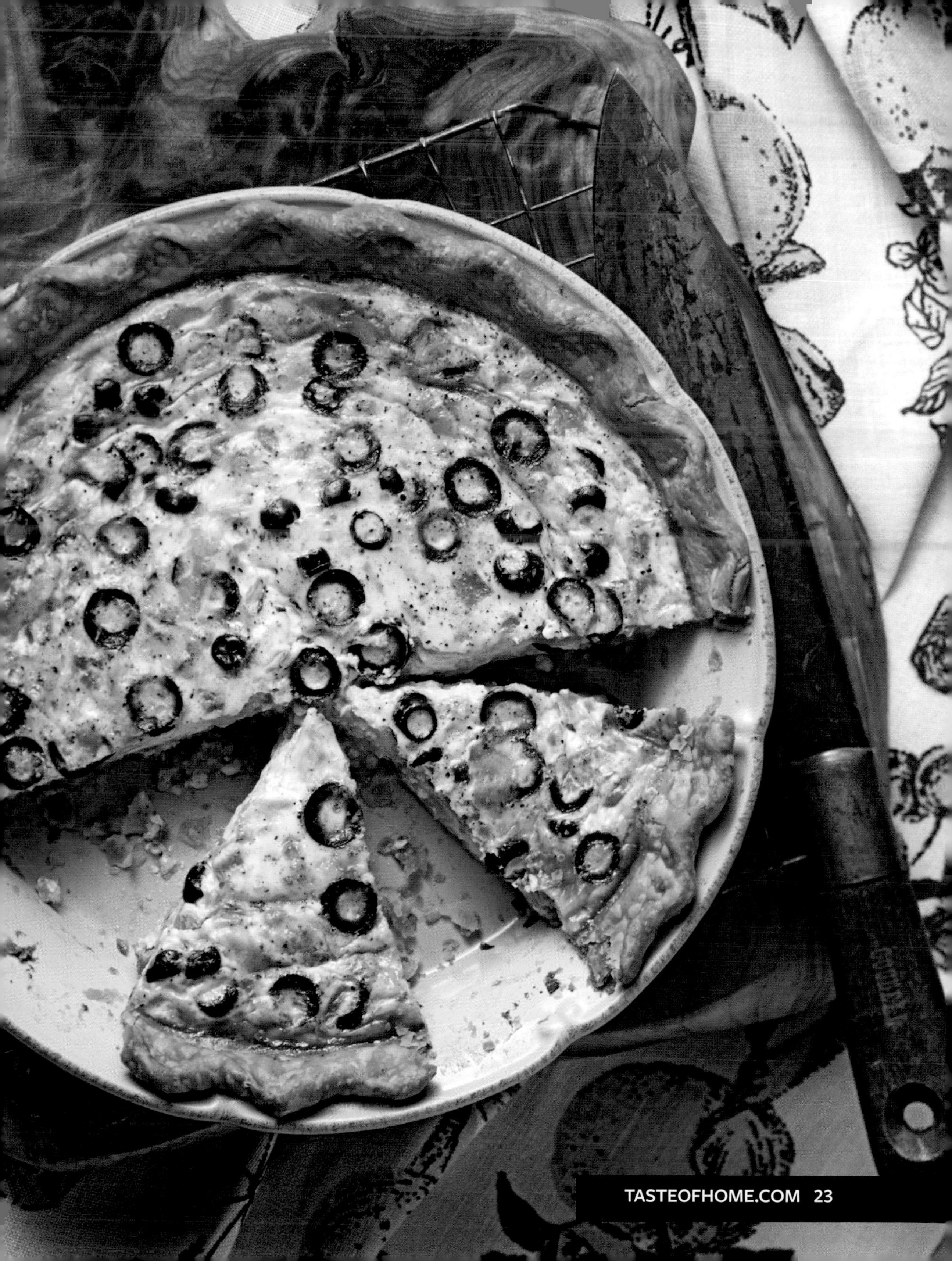

MORNING ORANGE DRINK

I treat my overnight guests to this creamy orange frappe. Just throw a few basic ingredients in your blender and enjoy.
—Joyce Mummau, Mount Airy, MD

TAKES: 10 min. • **MAKES:** 6 servings (about 1 qt.)

- 1 **can (6 oz.) frozen orange juice concentrate**
- 1 **cup cold water**
- 1 **cup whole milk**
- ⅓ **cup sugar**
- 1 **tsp. vanilla extract**
- 10 **ice cubes**

Combine the first 5 ingredients in a blender; process at high speed. Add ice cubes, a few at a time, blending until smooth. Serve immediately.

¾ CUP: 115 cal., 1g fat (1g sat. fat), 6mg chol., 21mg sod., 24g carb. (23g sugars, 0 fiber), 2g pro.

EGGS BENEDICT WITH HOMEMADE HOLLANDAISE

Legend has it that poached eggs on an English muffin started at Delmonico's in New York. Here's my take on this brunch classic, and don't spare the hollandaise.

—Barbara Pletzke, Herndon, VA

TAKES: 30 min. • **MAKES:** 8 servings

- 4 **large egg yolks**
- 2 **Tbsp. water**
- 2 **Tbsp. lemon juice**
- ¾ **cup butter, melted**
- **Dash white pepper**

ASSEMBLY

- 8 **large eggs**
- 4 **English muffins, split and toasted**
- 8 **slices Canadian bacon, warmed**
- **Paprika**

1. For hollandaise sauce, in top of a double boiler or a metal bowl over simmering water, whisk egg yolks, water and lemon juice until blended; cook until the mixture is just thick enough to coat a metal spoon and temperature reaches 160°, whisking constantly. Remove from heat. Very slowly drizzle in warm the melted butter, whisking constantly. Whisk in pepper. Transfer to a small bowl if necessary. Place the bowl in a larger bowl of warm water. Keep warm, stirring occasionally, until ready to serve, up to 30 minutes.

2. Place 2-3 in. of water in a large saucepan or skillet with high sides. Bring to a boil; adjust heat to maintain a gentle simmer. Break 1 egg into a small bowl; holding bowl close to surface of water, slip egg into water. Repeat with 3 more eggs.

3. Cook, uncovered, 2-4 minutes or until whites are completely set and yolks begin to thicken but are not hard. Using a slotted spoon, lift eggs out of water. Repeat with remaining 4 eggs.

4. Top each muffin half with a slice of bacon, a poached egg and 2 Tbsp. sauce; sprinkle with paprika. Serve immediately.

1 SERVING: 345 cal., 26g fat (14g sat. fat), 331mg chol., 522mg sod., 15g carb. (1g sugars, 1g fiber), 13g pro.

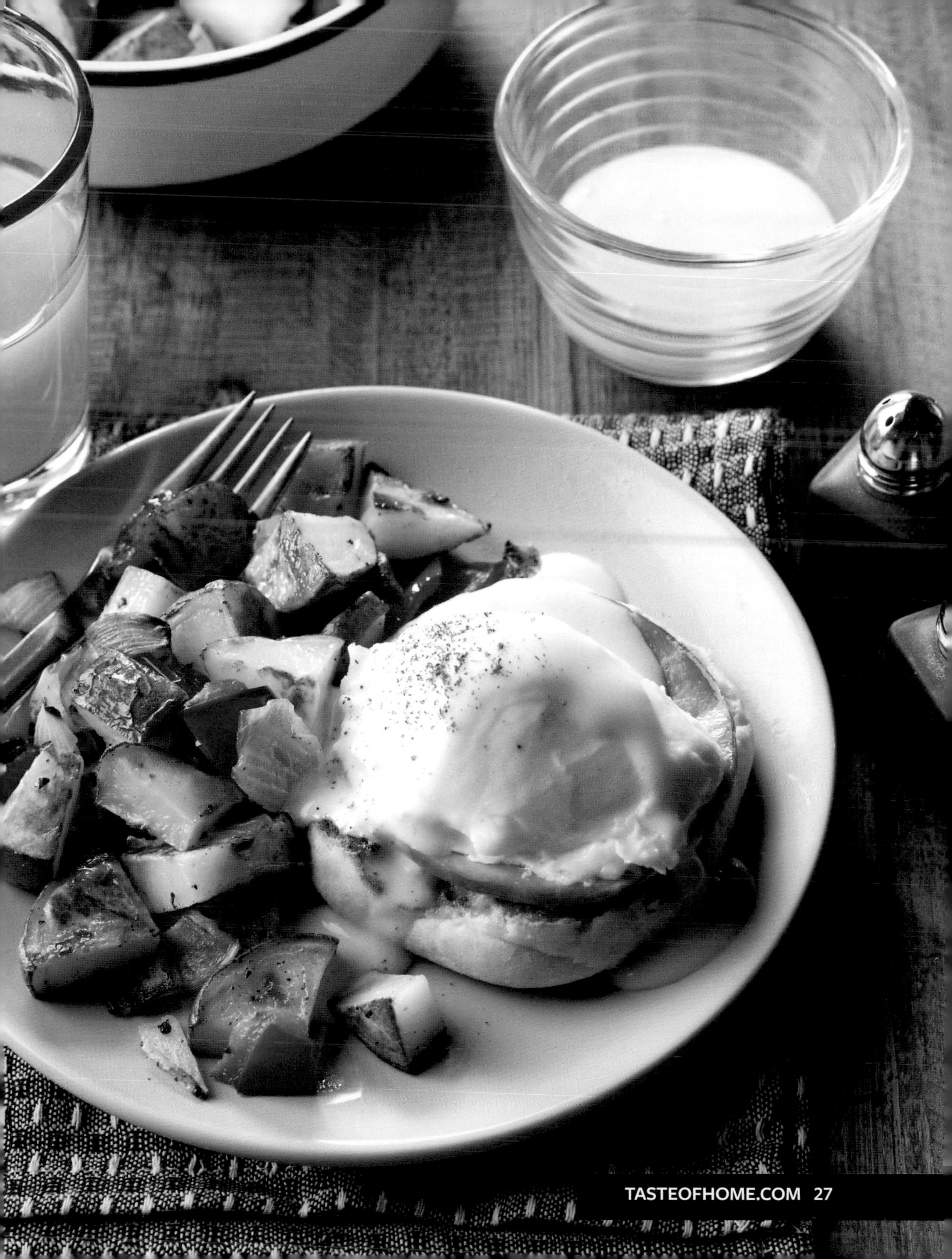

COFFEE-GLAZED DOUGHNUTS

The coffee-flavored glaze makes these doughnuts irresistible.
—Pat Siebenaler, Random Lake, WI

PREP: 25 min. + rising • **COOK:** 5 min./batch • **MAKES:** about 4 dozen

- 1 medium potato, peeled and cubed
- 2 pkg. (¼ oz. each) active dry yeast
- ¼ cup warm water (110° to 115°)
- 2 cups warm 2% milk (110° to 115°)
- ½ cup butter, softened
- 3 large eggs
- 1 cup sugar
- 1½ tsp. salt
- ½ tsp. ground cinnamon
- 9¼ to 9¾ cups all-purpose flour

COFFEE GLAZE
- 6 to 8 Tbsp. cold 2% milk
- 1 Tbsp. instant coffee granules
- 2 tsp. vanilla extract
- ¾ cup butter, softened
- 6 cups confectioners' sugar
- ½ tsp. ground cinnamon
- Dash salt
- Oil for deep-fat frying

1. Place potato in a medium saucepan; add water to cover. Bring to a boil. Reduce heat; cook, uncovered, until tender, 8-10 minutes. Drain potatoes; return to pan. Mash until very smooth.

2. In a bowl, dissolve yeast in warm water. Add the milk, butter, potato and eggs. Add sugar, salt, cinnamon and 3 cups flour. Beat until smooth. Stir in enough remaining flour to form a soft dough. Cover and let rise in a warm place until doubled, 1 hour.

3. Stir down dough. On a well-floured surface, roll out to ½-in. thickness. Cut with a floured 2½-in. doughnut cutter. Place on greased baking sheets; cover and let rise for 45 minutes.

4. For glaze, combine 6 Tbsp. milk, coffee and vanilla; stir to dissolve coffee. In a large bowl, beat the butter, sugar, cinnamon and salt. Gradually add milk mixture; beat until smooth, adding milk to reach desired dipping consistency.

5. In an electric skillet or deep-fat fryer, heat oil to 375°. Fry the doughnuts, a few at a time, until golden, 1½ minutes per side. Drain on paper towels. Dip tops in glaze while warm.

1 DOUGHNUT: 281 cal., 13g fat (4g sat. fat), 25mg chol., 127mg sod., 39g carb. (20g sugars, 1g fiber), 4g pro.

EASY GINGERBREAD PANCAKES

Simple yet scrumptious, these taste more like cake than breakfast pancakes. When I want to eat lighter, I top them with applesauce instead of butter and syrup.
—Trina Stewart, Yacolt, WA

PREP: 5 min. • **COOK:** 5 min./batch • **MAKES:** 12 pancakes

- 2 **cups complete pancake mix**
- 4 **tsp. molasses**
- ½ **tsp. ground cinnamon**
- ½ **tsp. ground ginger**
- ⅛ **tsp. ground cloves**
- 1½ **cups water**
  Maple syrup, optional

1. In a small bowl, combine the pancake mix, molasses, cinnamon, ginger and cloves. Stir in the water just until the dry ingredients are moistened.
2. Pour batter by ¼ cupfuls onto a greased hot griddle; turn when bubbles form on top. Cook until the second side is golden brown. Serve with syrup if desired.
3 PANCAKES: 248 cal., 2g fat (0 sat. fat), 0 chol., 972mg sod., 54g carb. (10g sugars, 1g fiber), 5g pro.

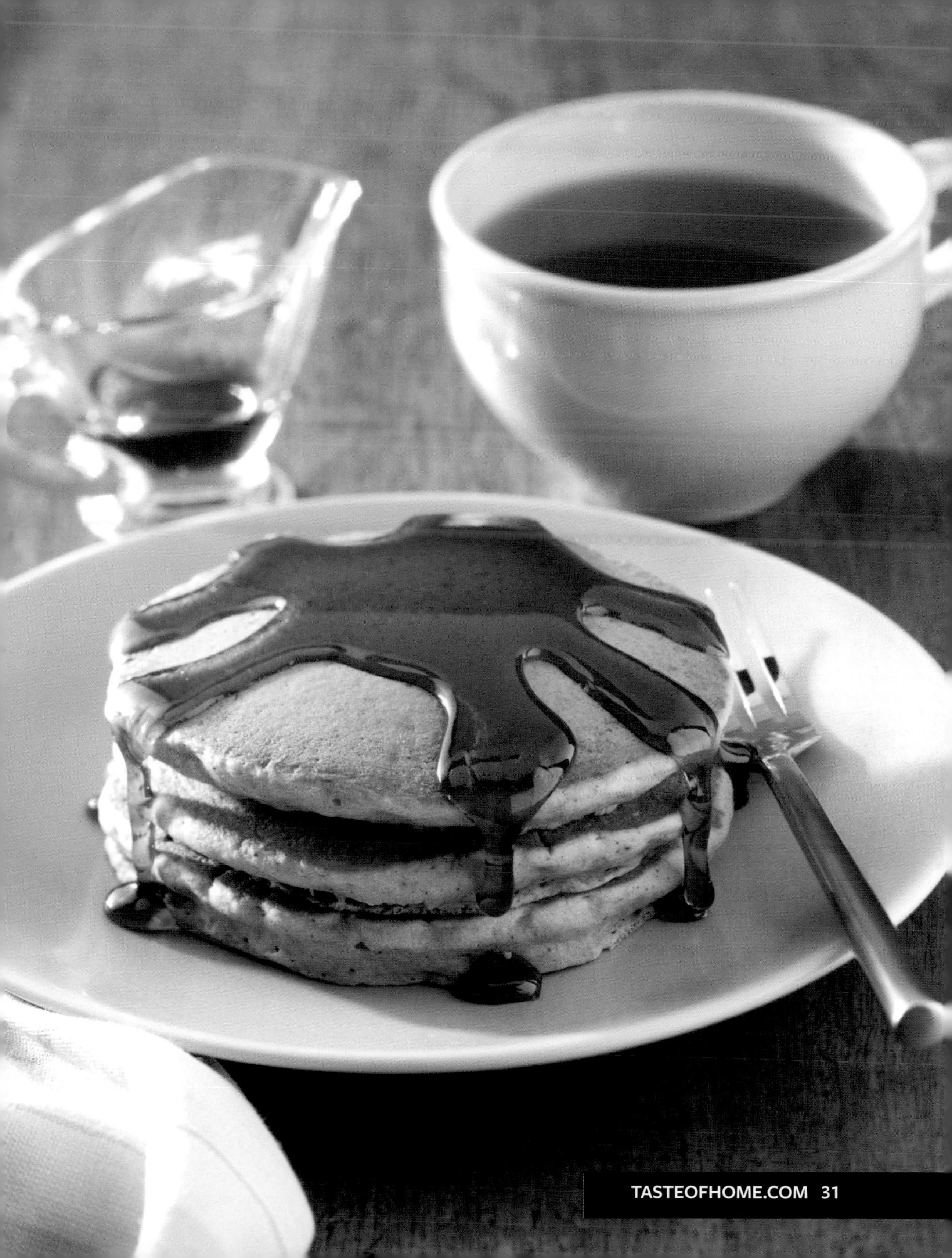

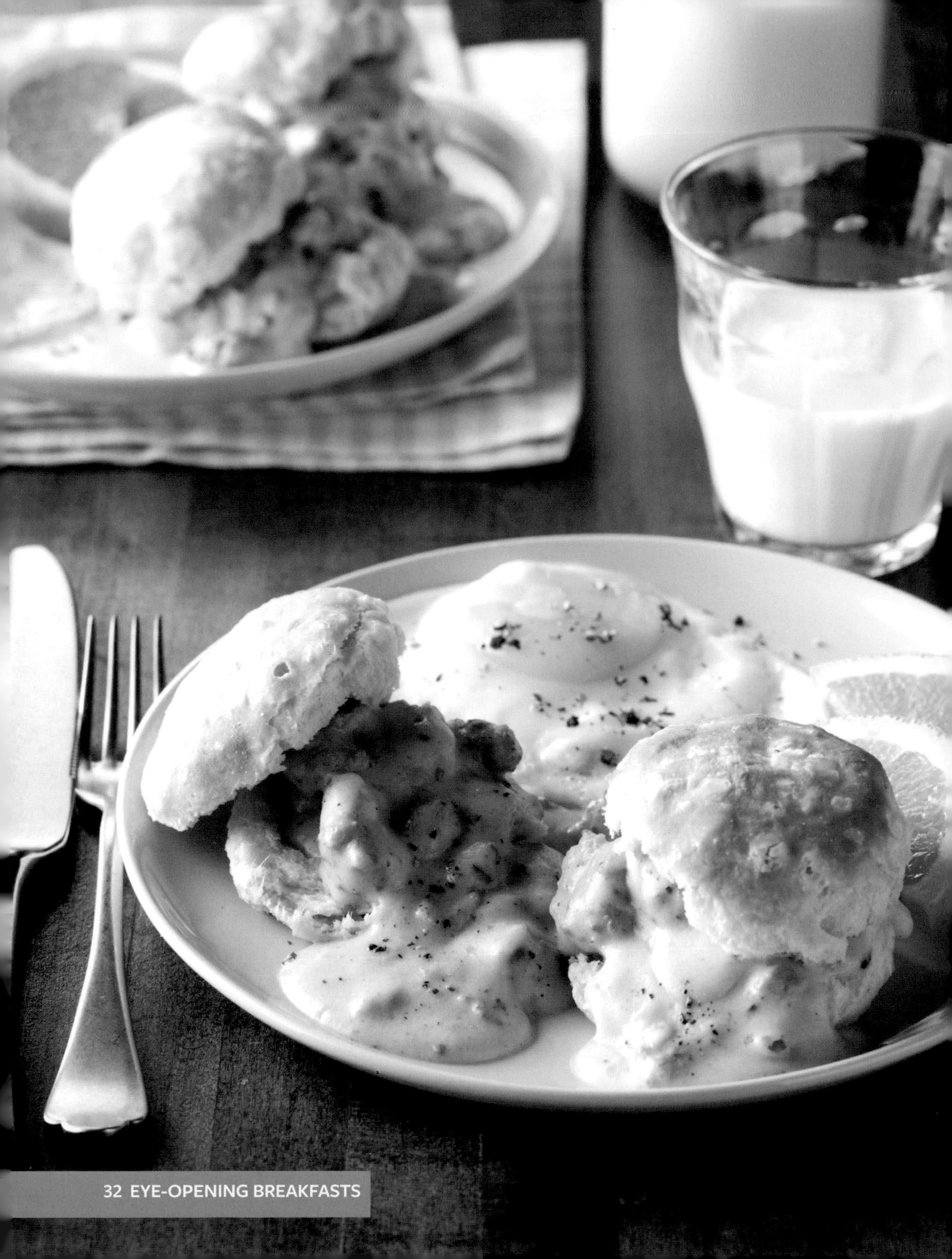

BISCUITS & SAUSAGE GRAVY

Here's a classic southern recipe I adapted to suit my tastes. It's the kind of hearty breakfast that warms you right up.
—Sue Baker, Jonesboro, AR

TAKES: 15 min. • **MAKES:** 2 servings

- ¼ lb. bulk pork sausage
- 2 Tbsp. butter
- 2 to 3 Tbsp. all-purpose flour
- ¼ tsp. salt
- ⅛ tsp. pepper
- 1¼ to 1⅓ cups whole milk
  Warm biscuits

In a small skillet, cook sausage over medium heat until no longer pink; drain. Add butter and heat until melted. Add the flour, salt and pepper; cook and stir until blended. Gradually add the milk, stirring constantly. Bring to a boil; cook and stir until thickened, about 2 minutes. Serve with biscuits.

¾ CUP GRAVY: 337 cal., 27g fat (14g sat. fat), 72mg chol., 718mg sod., 14g carb. (8g sugars, 0 fiber), 10g pro.

COUNTRY-STYLE SCRAMBLED EGGS

Add extra colors and flavors to ordinary scrambled eggs with green pepper, onion and red potatoes.
—Joyce Platfoot, Wapakoneta, OH

TAKES: 30 min. • **MAKES:** 4 servings

- 8 bacon strips, diced
- 2 cups diced red potatoes
- ½ cup chopped onion
- ½ cup chopped green pepper
- 8 large eggs
- ¼ cup whole milk
- 1 tsp. salt
- ¼ tsp. pepper
- 1 cup shredded cheddar cheese

1. In a 9-in. cast-iron or other ovenproof skillet, cook bacon over medium heat until crisp. Using a slotted spoon, remove to paper towels to drain. Cook and stir potatoes in drippings over medium heat for 12 minutes or until tender. Add onion and green pepper. Cook and stir for 3-4 minutes or until crisp-tender; drain. Stir in the bacon.
2. In a large bowl, whisk the eggs, milk, salt and pepper; add to skillet. Cook and stir until eggs are completely set. Sprinkle with cheese; stir it in or let stand until melted.
1 SERVING: 577 cal., 45g fat (19g sat. fat), 487mg chol., 1230mg sod., 18g carb. (4g sugars, 2g fiber), 25g pro.

CHEESE & GRITS CASSEROLE

Grits are a staple in southern cooking. Serve this as a brunch item with bacon and eggs or as a side dish for dinner.
—Jennifer Wallis, Goldsboro, NC

PREP: 10 min. • **BAKE:** 30 min. + standing • **MAKES:** 8 servings

- 4   cups water
- 1   cup uncooked old-fashioned grits
- ½   tsp. salt
- ½   cup 2% milk
- ¼   cup butter, melted
- 2   large eggs, lightly beaten
- 1   cup shredded cheddar cheese
- 1   Tbsp. Worcestershire sauce
- ⅛   tsp. cayenne pepper
- ⅛   tsp. paprika

1. Preheat oven to 350°. In a large saucepan, bring water to a boil. Slowly stir in grits and salt. Reduce heat, cover and simmer until thickened, 5-7 minutes. Cool slightly. Gradually whisk in the milk, butter and eggs. Stir in the cheddar cheese, Worcestershire sauce and cayenne.

2. Transfer to a greased 2-qt. baking dish. Sprinkle with paprika. Bake, uncovered, until bubbly, 30-35 minutes. Let stand for 10 minutes before serving.

¾ CUP: 202 cal., 12g fat (7g sat. fat), 86mg chol., 335mg sod., 17g carb. (1g sugars, 0 fiber), 7g pro.

TOAD IN THE HOLE

Here is one of the first recipes I taught my children when they were learning to cook. My little ones are now grown and have advanced to more difficult recipes, but this continues to be a standby in my home and theirs.
—Ruth Lechleiter, Breckenridge, MN

TAKES: 15 min. • **MAKES:** 1 serving

- 1   slice of bread
- 1   tsp. butter
- 1   large egg
     Salt and pepper to taste

1. Cut a 3-in. hole in the middle of the bread and discard. In a small skillet, melt the butter; place the bread in the skillet.
2. Place egg in the hole. Cook for about 2 minutes over medium heat until the bread is lightly browned. Turn and cook the other side until egg yolk is almost set. Season with salt and pepper.

1 SERVING: 183 cal., 10g fat (4g sat. fat), 196mg chol., 244mg sod., 15g carb. (2g sugars, 1g fiber), 9g pro.
DIABETIC EXCHANGES: 1 starch, 1 medium-fat meat, 1 fat.

Coffee Shop Favorites

LOVE YOUR MORNING PICK-ME-UP, BUT NOT THE PRICE? SAY GOODBYE TO EXPENSIVE CAFES AND HELLO TO YOUR OWN HOMEMADE COFFEE DRINKS! AND DON'T FORGET A SWEET BAKED TREAT TO GO WITH IT.

ICED COFFEE, P. 62

INSPIRED BY:
DUNKIN' DONUTS'
ICED COFFEE WITH
MOCHA FLAVOR SWIRL

INSPIRED BY:
**STARBUCKS'
BLUEBERRY SCONE**

BLUEBERRY SCONES

You'll want to stash a few of these homemade morsels in the freezer to serve to visitors who drop in unexpectedly. Just pop a frozen scone in the microwave for 20 seconds or so, and you have a warm treat.
—Joan Francis, Spring Lake, NJ

PREP: 20 min. • **BAKE:** 15 min. • **MAKES:** 16 scones

- 4 cups all-purpose flour
- 6 Tbsp. sugar
- 4½ tsp. baking powder
- ½ tsp. salt
- ½ cup plus 2 Tbsp. cold butter
- 2 large eggs, room temperature
- ¾ cup plus 2 Tbsp. whole milk, divided
- 1½ cups fresh or frozen blueberries

1. In a bowl, combine the flour, sugar, baking powder and salt; cut in butter until mixture resembles coarse crumbs. In a bowl, whisk eggs and ¾ cup milk; add to dry ingredients just until moistened. Turn onto a lightly floured surface; gently knead in the blueberries.
2. Divide the dough in half. Pat each portion into an 8-in. circle; cut each into 8 wedges. Place on greased baking sheets. Brush with remaining milk. Bake at 375° for 15-20 minutes or until tops are golden brown. Serve warm.
NOTE: If using frozen blueberries, use without thawing to avoid discoloring the batter.
1 SCONE: 220 cal., 9g fat (5g sat. fat), 48mg chol., 274mg sod., 31g carb. (7g sugars, 1g fiber), 5g pro.

GINGERBREAD HOT COCOA

Are you in the Christmas spirit yet? If not, this special cocoa will do the trick. It's like drinking a chocolate gingerbread cookie!
—Erika Monroe-Williams, Scottsdale, AZ

TAKES: 15 min. • **MAKES:** 3 servings

- ¼ cup packed brown sugar
- ¼ cup baking cocoa
- 1 Tbsp. molasses
- 1½ tsp. ground cinnamon
- 1½ tsp. ground ginger
- ½ tsp. ground allspice
  Pinch salt
- 3 cups whole milk
- 1 tsp. vanilla extract
  Whipped cream

In a small saucepan, combine the first 7 ingredients; gradually add milk. Cook and stir over medium heat until heated through. Remove from heat; stir in vanilla. Serve with whipped cream.
1 CUP: 269 cal., 9g fat (5g sat. fat), 24mg chol., 162mg sod., 41g carb. (35g sugars, 2g fiber), 9g pro.

INSPIRED BY:
IHOP'S
GINGERBREAD HOT CHOCOLATE

ASIAGO BAGELS

Discover a cheesy alternative to the usual sweet bread brunch offerings. There's no need to stop by a bakery when you can make bagels at home.
—Tami Kuehl, Loup City, NE

INSPIRED BY:
EINSTEIN BROS. BAGELS'
ASIAGO CHEESE BAGEL

PREP: 30 min. + standing • **BAKE:** 15 min. + cooling
MAKES: 1 dozen

- 1 cup water (70° to 80°)
- 2 large eggs, room temperature
- ¼ cup plus 1 Tbsp. olive oil
- 2 Tbsp. honey
- ¾ cup shredded Asiago cheese, divided
- ⅓ cup nonfat dry milk powder
- 1½ tsp. salt
- 1 tsp. dried basil
- 2 cups whole wheat flour
- 1½ cups plus 2 Tbsp. all-purpose flour
- 4 tsp. active dry yeast
- 1 large egg white
- 1 Tbsp. water

1. In bread machine pan, place the water, eggs, oil, honey, ½ cup Asiago cheese, milk powder, salt, basil, flours and yeast in order suggested by manufacturer. Select the dough setting (check the dough after 5 minutes of mixing; add 1 to 2 Tbsp. of water or flour if needed).

2. When cycle is completed, turn dough onto a lightly floured surface. Shape into 12 balls. Push thumb through centers to form a 1½-in. hole. Stretch and shape dough to form an even ring. Cover and let rest for 10 minutes; flatten bagels slightly.

3. Fill a Dutch oven two-thirds full with water; bring to a boil. Drop bagels, 2 at a time, into boiling water. Cook for 45 seconds; turn and cook 45 seconds longer. Remove with a slotted spoon; drain well on paper towels.

4. In a small bowl, combine egg white and water; brush over bagels. Sprinkle with remaining cheese. Place 2 in. apart on greased baking sheets. Bake at 400° for 15-20 minutes or until golden brown. Remove to wire racks to cool.

1 BAGEL: 239 cal., 9g fat (2g sat. fat), 42mg chol., 342mg sod., 32g carb. (5g sugars, 3g fiber), 9g pro
DIABETIC EXCHANGES: 2 starch, 1 fat.

CREAMY CARAMEL MOCHA

Indulge in a coffeehouse quality drink at Christmastime or any time a craving calls. With whipped cream and a butterscotch drizzle, this mocha treat will perk up even the sleepiest person at the table.
—*Taste of Home* Test Kitchen

TAKES: 20 min. • **MAKES:** 6 servings (1½ qt.)

- ½ cup heavy whipping cream
- 1 Tbsp. confectioners' sugar
- 1 tsp. vanilla extract, divided
- ¼ cup Dutch-processed cocoa
- 1½ cups half-and-half cream
- 4 cups hot strong brewed coffee
- ½ cup caramel flavoring syrup
  Butterscotch-caramel ice cream topping

1. In a small bowl, beat whipping cream until it begins to thicken. Add confectioners' sugar and ½ tsp. vanilla extract; beat until stiff peaks form.

2. In a large saucepan over medium heat, whisk cocoa and half-and-half cream until smooth. Heat until bubbles form around sides of pan. Whisk in coffee, caramel syrup and remaining vanilla. Top servings with whipped cream; drizzle with butterscotch topping.

3. To prepare in a slow cooker: Prepare whipped cream as directed. Whisk together cocoa, half-and-half, coffee, caramel syrup and remaining vanilla in a 3-qt. slow cooker. Cook, covered, 2-3 hours or until heated through. Serve as directed.

NOTE: This recipe was tested with Torani brand flavoring syrup. Look for it in the coffee section.

1 CUP COFFEE WITH 2 TBSP. WHIPPED CREAM: 220 cal., 14g fat (9g sat. fat), 57mg chol., 38mg sod., 19g carb. (16g sugars, 1g fiber), 3g pro.

WARM SPICED CHAI

My wife and I enjoy a hot cup of chai, but I have never been satisfied with any of the store-bought mixes. So I created my own!
—Justin Weber, Milwaukee, WI

TAKES: 25 min. • **MAKES:** 6 servings (1½ qt.)

- 6 cardamom pods
- ½ tsp. whole peppercorns
- 5 cups water
- ¼ cup honey
- 2 cinnamon sticks (3 in.)
- 8 whole cloves
- 3 whole star anise
- 1 Tbsp. minced fresh gingerroot
- 5 black tea bags
- 2 cups whole milk
- 1 Tbsp. vanilla extract
   Ground nutmeg, optional

1. In a spice grinder or with a mortar and pestle, combine cardamom pods and peppercorns; grind until aromas are released.
2. In a large saucepan, bring water to boil. Add cardamom mixture, honey, cinnamon sticks, cloves, star anise and ginger; simmer 5 minutes or according to taste. Remove from heat. Add tea bags; cover and steep 5 minutes.
3. Meanwhile, in a small saucepan, heat milk. Strain tea, discarding spices and tea bags. Stir in hot milk and vanilla. Pour into mugs. If desired, sprinkle with nutmeg.
1 CUP: 102 cal., 3g fat (2g sat. fat), 8mg chol., 44mg sod., 17g carb. (16g sugars, 1 fiber), 3g pro.

HOLIDAY PEPPERMINT MOCHA

Making this for a group on a snowy night doesn't take any more time than it takes to make it for one.
—Lauren Brien-Wooster, South Lake Tahoe, CA

TAKES: 10 min. • **MAKES:** 8 servings

- 4 cups 2% milk
- 8 packets instant hot cocoa mix
- 1½ cups brewed espresso or double-strength dark roast coffee
- ¾ cup peppermint schnapps liqueur or 1 tsp. peppermint extract plus ¾ cup additional brewed espresso
  Whipped cream, optional

1. In a large saucepan, heat milk over medium heat until bubbles form around sides of pan. Add cocoa mix; whisk until blended. Add espresso and heat through.

2. Remove from heat; stir in the liqueur. If desired, serve with whipped cream.

¾ CUP: 197 cal., 6g fat (4g sat. fat), 10mg chol., 234mg sod., 22g carb. (18g sugars, 1g fiber), 5g pro.

INSPIRED BY:
**DUNKIN' DONUTS'
PEPPERMINT MOCHA**

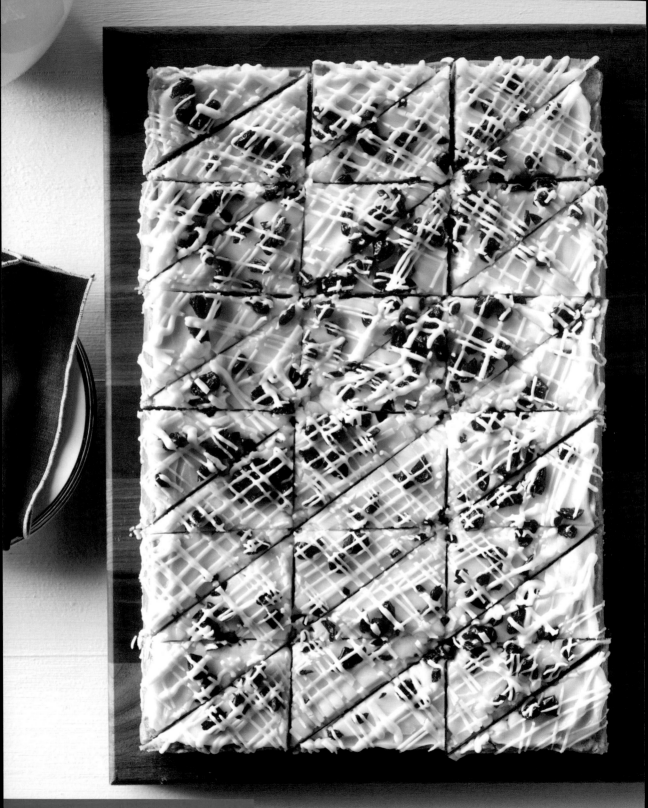

WHITE CHOCOLATE CRANBERRY BLONDIES

My family often requests these bars. For a fancier presentation, cut them into triangles and drizzle melted white chocolate over each one individually.
—Erika Busz, Kent, WA

PREP: 35 min. • **BAKE:** 20 min. + cooling • **MAKES:** 3 dozen

- ¾ cup butter, cubed
- 1½ cups packed light brown sugar
- 2 large eggs, room temperature
- ¾ tsp. vanilla extract
- 2¼ cups all-purpose flour
- 1½ tsp. baking powder
- ¼ tsp. salt
- ⅛ tsp. ground cinnamon
- ½ cup dried cranberries
- 6 oz. white baking chocolate, coarsely chopped

FROSTING

- 1 pkg. (8 oz.) cream cheese, softened
- 1 cup confectioners' sugar
- 1 Tbsp. grated orange zest, optional
- 6 oz. white baking chocolate, melted
- ½ cup dried cranberries, chopped

1. Preheat oven to 350°. In a large microwave-safe bowl, melt the butter; stir in the brown sugar. Cool slightly.
2. Beat in 1 egg at a time, and vanilla. In another bowl, whisk together flour, baking powder, salt and cinnamon; stir into butter mixture. Stir in cranberries and chopped chocolate (batter will be thick). Spread into a greased 13x9-in. pan.
3. Bake until golden brown and a toothpick inserted in center comes out clean (do not overbake), 18-21 minutes. Cool completely on a wire rack.
4. For frosting, beat cream cheese, confectioners' sugar and, if desired, orange zest until smooth. Gradually beat in half of the melted white chocolate; spread over blondies. Sprinkle with cranberries; drizzle with remaining melted chocolate.
5. Cut into triangles. Store blondies in an airtight container in the refrigerator.

1 BLONDIE: 198 cal., 9g fat (6g sat. fat), 27mg chol., 100mg sod., 28g carb. (22g sugars, 0 fiber), 2g pro.

INSPIRED BY:
STARBUCKS'
CRANBERRY BLISS BAR

INSPIRED BY:
EINSTEIN BROS. BAGELS'
FROZEN PUMPKIN LATTE

SPICED PUMPKIN COFFEE SHAKES

The winter holidays are my favorite time of year, and this spiced pumpkin drink is one reason I love the season so much. If you don't have a coffee maker, use instant coffee—just make it stronger.
—Kathie Perez, East Peoria, IL

PREP: 15 min. + chilling • **MAKES:** 6 servings

- 2 **cups whole milk**
- ½ **cup canned pumpkin**
- 2 **Tbsp. sugar**
- 1 **tsp. pumpkin pie spice**
- 1 **cup strong brewed coffee**
- 3 **tsp. vanilla extract**
- 4 **cups vanilla ice cream**
- 1 **cup crushed ice**
  Sweetened whipped cream and additional pumpkin pie spice

1. In a small saucepan, heat milk, pumpkin, sugar and pie spice until bubbles form around sides of pan and sugar is dissolved. Transfer to a bowl; stir in coffee and vanilla. Refrigerate, covered, several hours or overnight.

2. Place milk mixture, ice cream and ice in a blender; cover and process until blended. Serve immediately with whipped cream; sprinkle with additional pie spice.

1 SERVING: 262 cal., 12g fat (8g sat. fat), 47mg chol., 107mg sod., 31g carb. (28g sugars, 1g fiber), 6g pro.

PUMPKIN DOUGHNUT DROPS

I always have a few special treats handy when the grandchildren visit. These cake doughnuts are one of their favorite snacks.
—Beva Staum, Muscoda, WI

PREP: 10 min. • **COOK:** 5 min./batch • **MAKES:** about 7 dozen

- 2 **large eggs**
- 1¼ **cups sugar**
- 2 **Tbsp. shortening**
- 1 **cup canned pumpkin**
- 2 **tsp. white vinegar**
- 1 **tsp. vanilla extract**
- 3 **cups all-purpose flour**
- ½ **cup nonfat dry milk powder**
- 3 **tsp. baking powder**
- ½ **tsp. salt**
- ½ **tsp. ground cinnamon**
- ½ **tsp. ground nutmeg**
- ½ **cup lemon-lime soda**
  Oil for deep-fat frying
  Additional sugar

1. In a large bowl, beat eggs, sugar and shortening until blended. Beat in the pumpkin, vinegar and vanilla. In another bowl, whisk together flour, milk powder, baking powder, salt and spices. Add to egg mixture alternately with soda, beating after each addition.
2. In an electric skillet or deep fryer, heat oil to 375°. Drop teaspoonfuls of batter, a few at a time, into hot oil. Fry until golden brown, about 1 minute per side. Drain on paper towels. Roll in additional sugar while warm.

1 DOUGHNUT DROP: 48 cal., 2g fat (0 sat. fat), 5mg chol., 36mg sod., 7g carb. (3g sugars, 0 fiber), 1g pro.

AUNT BETTY'S BLUEBERRY MUFFINS

My Aunt Betty is famous for her baked goods. I look forward to these mouthwatering muffins the most, especially around the holidays.
—Sheila Raleigh, Kechi, KS

PREP: 15 min. • **BAKE:** 20 min. • **MAKES:** about 1 dozen

- ½ cup old-fashioned oats
- ½ cup orange juice
- 1 large egg, room temperature
- ½ cup canola oil
- ½ cup sugar
- 1½ cups all-purpose flour
- 1¼ tsp. baking powder
- ½ tsp. salt
- ¼ tsp. baking soda
- 1 cup fresh or frozen blueberries

TOPPING

- 2 Tbsp. sugar
- ½ tsp. ground cinnamon

1. In a large bowl, combine oats and orange juice; let stand for 5 minutes. Beat in the egg, oil and sugar until blended. Combine the flour, baking powder, salt and baking soda; stir into oat mixture just until moistened. Fold in blueberries.

2. Fill greased or paper-lined muffin cups two-thirds full. Combine topping ingredients; sprinkle over batter. Bake at 400° until a toothpick inserted in the center comes out clean, 20-25 minutes. Cool muffins for 5 minutes before removing from pan to a wire rack. Serve warm.

NOTE: If using frozen blueberries, use without thawing to avoid discoloring the batter.

1 MUFFIN: 208 cal., 10g fat (1g sat. fat), 18mg chol., 172mg sod., 28g carb. (13g sugars, 1g fiber), 3g pro.

INSPIRED BY:
STARBUCKS'
HAZELNUT FRAPPUCCINO

HAZELNUT MOCHA FRAPPUCCINO

This smooth blend of coffee, cocoa and nutty flavors is better than any coffeehouse version we've tried. Try it, and you'll agree.
—*Taste of Home* Test Kitchen

TAKES: 10 min. • **MAKES:** 3 servings

- 1 **cup whole milk**
- ½ **cup Nutella**
- 4 **tsp. instant espresso powder**
- 6 **ice cubes**
- 2 **cups vanilla ice cream**
  Chocolate curls, optional

In a blender, combine the milk, Nutella and espresso powder; cover and process until blended. Add ice cubes; cover and process until smooth. Add ice cream; cover and process until smooth. Pour into chilled glasses; serve immediately. Garnish with chocolate curls if desired.
1 CUP: 474 cal., 27g fat (10g sat. fat), 47mg chol., 124mg sod., 55g carb. (46g sugars, 2g fiber), 9g pro.

PEPPERMINT WHITE HOT CHOCOLATE

My soothing white hot chocolate is a great warmup after a wintry day spent sledding or ice skating.
—Darlene Brenden, Salem, OR

TAKES: 15 min. • **MAKES:** 6 servings (1½ qt.)

5½ cups 2% milk
⅓ cup heavy whipping cream
4 tsp. crushed peppermint candies, divided
12 oz. white baking chocolate, chopped
¾ tsp. peppermint extract
   Miniature marshmallows, optional

1. In a large saucepan, heat milk over medium heat until bubbles form around sides of pan. Meanwhile, in a small bowl, beat cream until stiff peaks form. Fold in 1 tsp. crushed candy.
2. Whisk chocolate into milk until smooth. Remove from heat; stir in extract. Pour into mugs; top with whipped cream. Sprinkle with remaining candy and, if desired, marshmallows. Serve immediately.
1 CUP WITH ABOUT 1 TBSP. WHIPPED CREAM AND ½ TSP. CRUSHED CANDY: 519 cal., 32g fat (19g sat. fat), 54mg chol., 153mg sod., 46g carb. (44g sugars, 0 fiber), 11g pro.

LEMON POUND CAKE LOAVES

The next time you're spending the weekend at a friend's house, take these luscious lemon loaves with you and enjoy them for breakfast in the morning. Your host will definitely invite you back for a future visit!
—Lola Baxter, Winnebago, MN

PREP: 20 min. • **BAKE:** 35 min. + cooling
MAKES: 2 mini loaves (6 slices each)

- ½ cup butter, softened
- 1 cup sugar
- 2 large eggs, room temperature
- 1 tsp. grated lemon zest
- 1 tsp. vanilla extract
- ½ tsp. lemon extract
- 1¾ cups all-purpose flour
- ½ tsp. salt
- ¼ tsp. baking soda
- ½ cup sour cream

ICING
- ¾ cup confectioners' sugar
- ½ tsp. grated lemon zest
- 1 Tbsp. lemon juice

1. Preheat the oven to 350°. Grease and flour two 5¾x3x2-in. loaf pans.

2. In a large bowl, cream butter and sugar until light and fluffy. Add 1 egg at a time, beating well after each addition. Beat in the lemon zest and extracts. In another bowl, whisk the flour, salt and baking soda; add to creamed mixture alternately with sour cream, beating well after each addition.

3. Transfer to prepared pans. Bake 35-40 minutes or until a toothpick inserted in center comes out clean. Cool in pans 10 minutes before removing to wire racks to cool completely.

4. In a small bowl, mix icing ingredients. Spoon over loaves.

FREEZE OPTION: Do not make icing. Securely wrap cooled loaves in plastic wrap and foil, then freeze. To use, thaw loaves at room temperature. Prepare icing as directed.

1 SLICE: 262 cal., 10g fat (6g sat. fat), 58mg chol., 201mg sod., 39g carb. (25g sugars, 1g fiber), 3g pro.

FOR ONE LARGE LOAF: Make batter as directed; transfer to a greased and floured 8x4-in. loaf pan. Bake in a preheated 350° oven for 40-45 minutes or until a toothpick comes out clean. Proceed as directed. Yield: 1 loaf (12 slices).

ICED COFFEE

When my sister introduced me to iced coffee, I wasn't sure I'd like it. Not only did I love it, I started making my own. This easy version is a refreshing alternative to hot coffee.
—Jenny Reece, Lowry, MN

TAKES: 5 min. • **MAKES:** 2 cups

   4   **tsp. instant coffee granules**
   1   **cup boiling water**
       Sugar substitute equivalent to 4 tsp. sugar, optional
   1   **cup fat-free milk**
   4   **tsp. chocolate syrup**
   ⅛   **tsp. vanilla extract**
       Ice cubes

In a large bowl, dissolve coffee in water. Add sweetener if desired. Stir in the milk, chocolate syrup and vanilla; mix well. Serve over ice.
NOTE: This recipe was tested with Splenda no-calorie sweetener.
1 CUP: 80 cal., 0 fat (0 sat. fat), 2mg chol., 60mg sod., 15g carb. (13g sugars, 0 fiber), 5g pro.
DIABETIC EXCHANGES: ½ starch, ½ fat-free milk.

PUMPKIN SPICE LATTE

Each sip of this spiced-just-right beverage from our home economists tastes like a piece of pumpkin pie!
—*Taste of Home* Test Kitchen

TAKES: 20 min. • **MAKES:** 6 servings

- 3 **cups 2% milk**
- ¾ **cup canned pumpkin**
- ⅓ **cup packed brown sugar**
- ½ **tsp. ground cinnamon**
- ¼ **tsp. ground ginger**
- ⅛ **tsp. ground nutmeg**
- 1½ **cups hot brewed espresso or strong brewed dark roast coffee**
  Optiona: Whipped cream and additional nutmeg

Place first 6 ingredients in a large saucepan. Cook and stir over medium heat until heated through. Stir in hot espresso. Pour into warm mugs. If desired, top with whipped cream and additional ground nutmeg.

1 SERVING: 124 cal., 3g fat (2g sat. fat), 10mg chol., 71mg sod., 22g carb. (19g sugars, 1g fiber), 4g pro.

CINNAMON BAGELS WITH CRUNCHY TOPPING

Once you get the hang of it, you won't believe how simple it is to make these bakery-quality bagels right in your own kitchen.
—Kristen Streepey, Geneva, IL

PREP: 40 min. + rising • **BAKE:** 15 min. + cooling • **MAKES:** 1 dozen

- 2 tsp. active dry yeast
- 1½ cups warm water (110° to 115°)
- 4 Tbsp. brown sugar, divided
- 3 tsp. ground cinnamon
- 1½ tsp. salt
- 2¾ to 3¼ cups all-purpose flour

TOPPING
- ¼ cup sugar
- ¼ cup packed brown sugar
- 3 tsp. ground cinnamon

1. In a large bowl, dissolve yeast in warm water. Add 3 Tbsp. brown sugar, cinnamon and salt; mix well. Stir in enough flour to form a soft dough.

2. Turn onto a lightly floured surface; knead until smooth and elastic, about 6-8 minutes. Place in a bowl coated with cooking spray, turning once to coat the top. Cover and let rise in a warm place until doubled, about 1 hour.

3. Punch dough down. Shape into 12 balls. Push thumb through each center to form a 1½-in. hole. Stretch and shape dough to form an even ring. Place on a floured surface. Cover dough rings and let rest for 10 minutes.

4. Fill a Dutch oven two-thirds full with water and remaining brown sugar; bring to a boil. Drop bagels, 2 at a time, into boiling water. Cook for 45 seconds; turn and cook 45 seconds longer. Remove with a slotted spoon; drain well on paper towels.

5. In a small bowl, mix topping ingredients; sprinkle over bagels. Place 2 in. apart on baking sheets coated with cooking spray. Bake at 400° for 15-20 minutes or until golden brown. Remove to wire racks to cool.

1 BAGEL: 164 cal., 0 fat (0 sat. fat), 0 chol., 300mg sod., 37g carb. (14g sugars, 2g fiber), 4g pro.

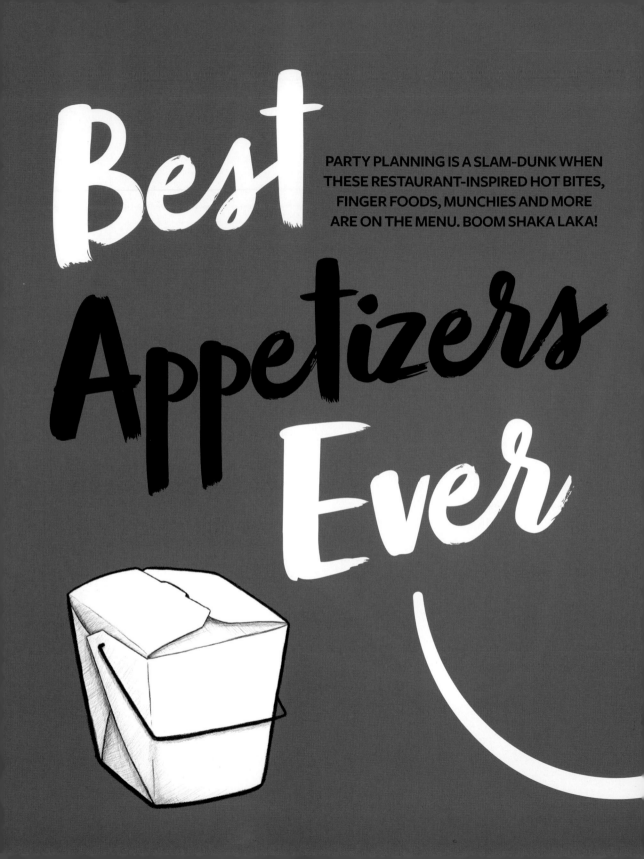

Best Appetizers Ever

PARTY PLANNING IS A SLAM-DUNK WHEN THESE RESTAURANT-INSPIRED HOT BITES, FINGER FOODS, MUNCHIES AND MORE ARE ON THE MENU. BOOM SHAKA LAKA!

ASIAN CHICKEN DUMPLINGS, P. 97
INSPIRED BY:
CALIFORNIA PIZZA KITCHEN'S
SZECHWAN CHICKEN DUMPLINGS

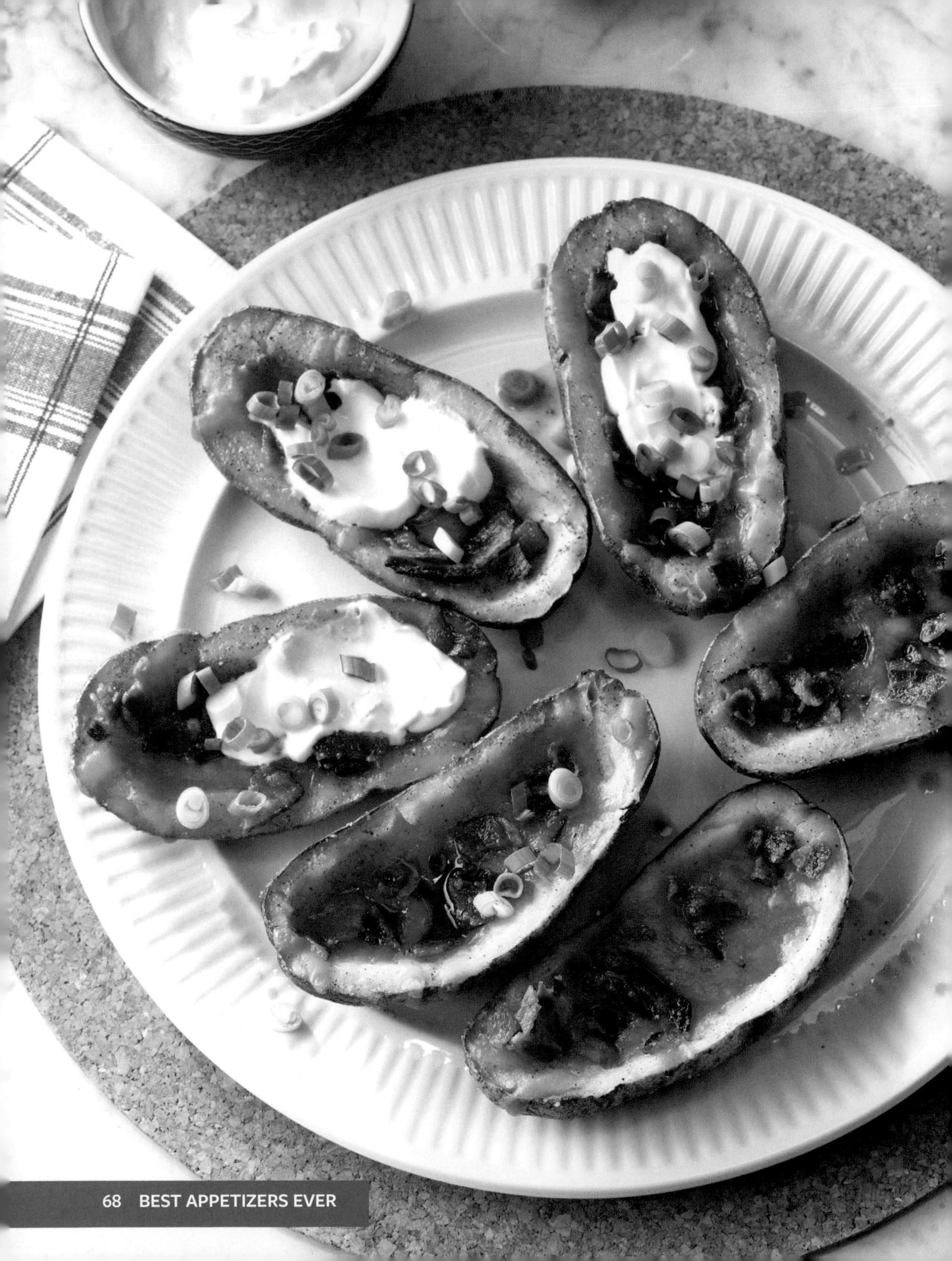

BACON CHEDDAR POTATO SKINS

Thank goodness it's tater time! My take on the classic app bakes up crisp and hearty. It's one of our family's favorites.
—Trish Perrin, Keizer, OR

TAKES: 30 min. • **MAKES:** 8 servings

- 4 large baking potatoes, baked
- 3 Tbsp. canola oil
- 1 Tbsp. grated Parmesan cheese
- ½ tsp. salt
- ¼ tsp. garlic powder
- ¼ tsp. paprika
- ⅛ tsp. pepper
- 8 bacon strips, cooked and crumbled
- 1½ cups shredded cheddar cheese
- ½ cup sour cream
- 4 green onions, sliced

1. Preheat oven to 475°. Cut potatoes in half lengthwise; scoop out pulp, leaving a ¼-in. shell (save pulp for another use). Place potato skins on a greased baking sheet.
2. Combine oil with the next 5 ingredients; brush over both sides of skins.
3. Bake until crisp, about 7 minutes on each side. Sprinkle bacon and cheddar cheese inside skins. Bake until cheese is melted, about 2 minutes longer. Top with sour cream and onions. Serve immediately.

1 POTATO SKIN: 350 cal., 19g fat (7g sat. fat), 33mg chol., 460mg sod., 34g carb. (2g sugars, 4g fiber), 12g pro.

INSPIRED BY:
**TGI FRIDAYS'
LOADED POTATO SKINS**

HAVE IT YOUR WAY
Cut down your kitchen time: Instead of prebaking the potatoes in an oven for 50-60 minutes, microwave them for 4 minutes. Scoop out the pulp, then make the potato skins as directed.

SOFT GIANT PRETZELS

My husband, friends and family love these soft, chewy pretzels. Let your machine mix the dough, then just shape and bake.
—Sherry Peterson, Fort Collins, CO

PREP: 20 min. + rising • **BAKE:** 10 min. • **MAKES:** 8 pretzels

- 1 cup plus 2 Tbsp. water (70° to 80°)
- 3 cups all-purpose flour
- 3 Tbsp. brown sugar
- 1½ tsp. active dry yeast
- 2 qt. water
- ½ cup baking soda
  Coarse salt

1. In bread machine pan, place the first 4 ingredients in order suggested by manufacturer. Select dough setting (check the dough after 5 minutes of mixing; add 1 to 2 Tbsp. water or flour if needed).

2. When cycle is completed, turn dough onto a lightly floured surface. Divide dough into 8 balls. Roll each into a 20-in. rope; form into pretzel shape.

3. Preheat oven to 425°. In a large saucepan, bring water and baking soda to a boil. Drop pretzels into boiling water, 2 at a time; boil for 10-15 seconds. Remove with a slotted spoon; drain on paper towels.

4. Place pretzels on greased baking sheets. Bake until golden brown, 8-10 minutes. Spritz or lightly brush with water. Sprinkle with salt.

1 PRETZEL: 193 cal., 1g fat (0 sat. fat), 0 chol., 380mg sod., 41g carb. (5g sugars, 1g fiber), 5g pro.

CHICKEN QUESADILLAS

Lightly baked to cheesy, melty perfection, these quesadillas are a winner for celebrations, big and small. They make a great weeknight dish, too.
—Linda Wetzel, Woodland Park, CO

TAKES: 30 min. • **MAKES:** 6 servings

- 2½ cups shredded cooked chicken
- ⅔ cup salsa
- ⅓ cup sliced green onions
- ¾ to 1 tsp. ground cumin
- ½ tsp. salt
- ½ tsp. dried oregano
- 6 flour tortillas (8 in.)
- ¼ cup butter, melted
- 2 cups shredded Monterey Jack cheese
  Sour cream and guacamole

1. In a large skillet, combine the first 6 ingredients. Cook, uncovered, over medium heat until heated through, about 10 minutes, stirring occasionally.
2. Brush 1 side of tortillas with butter; place buttered side down on a lightly greased baking sheet. Spoon ⅓ cup chicken mixture over half of each tortilla; sprinkle with ⅓ cup cheese.
3. Fold plain side of tortilla over cheese. Bake at 375° until crisp and golden brown, 9-11 minutes. Cut into wedges; serve with sour cream and guacamole.
1 SERVING: 477 cal., 26g fat (13g sat. fat), 106mg chol., 901mg sod., 27g carb. (1g sugars, 1g fiber), 31g pro.

INSPIRED BY:
**APPLEBEE'S
CHICKEN QUESADILLA**

HAVE IT YOUR WAY

Feel free to add your favorite taco toppings, such as tomatoes, bell peppers, corn or jalapenos, inside this quesadilla. Just be sure to not overstuff the tortilla. You don't want your ingredients to ooze out during baking!

INSPIRED BY:
CALIFORNIA PIZZA KITCHEN'S
ROASTED ARTICHOKE
+ SPINACH PIZZA

ARTICHOKE & SPINACH DIP PIZZA

When I have it in my pantry, I swap garlic oil for regular olive oil. It adds a little something without overpowering the toppings.
—Shelly Bevington, Hermiston, OR

TAKES: 20 min. • **MAKES:** 24 pieces

- 1 prebaked 12-in. pizza crust
- 1 Tbsp. olive oil
- 1 cup spinach dip
- 1 cup shredded part-skim mozzarella cheese
- 1 jar (7½ oz.) marinated quartered artichoke hearts, drained
- ½ cup oil-packed sun-dried tomatoes, patted dry and chopped
- ¼ cup chopped red onion

1. Preheat oven to 450°. Place crust on an ungreased pizza pan; brush with oil. Spread spinach dip over top. Sprinkle with cheese, artichokes, tomatoes and onion.
2. Bake until cheese is melted and edges of crust are lightly browned, 8-10 minutes. Cut into 24 pieces.
1 PIECE: 127 cal., 9g fat (2g sat. fat), 6mg chol., 213mg sod., 10g carb. (1g sugars, 0 fiber), 3g pro.

HONEY MUSTARD CHICKEN WINGS

Take a walk on the wild side with these sweet and sticky wings. They're a fun flavor twist from traditional spicy Buffalo sauce.
—Susan Seymour, Valatie, NY

PREP: 15 min. • **BAKE:** 1 hour • **MAKES:** about 3 dozen

- 4 lbs. chicken wings
- ½ cup spicy brown mustard
- ½ cup honey
- ¼ cup butter, cubed
- 2 Tbsp. lemon juice
- ¼ tsp. ground turmeric

1. Preheat oven to 400°. Line two 15x10x1-in. baking pans with foil; grease foil. Using a sharp knife, cut through the 2 chicken wing joints; discard wing tips. Place remaining wings in prepared pans.

2. In a small saucepan, combine remaining ingredients; bring to a boil, stirring frequently. Pour over wings, turning to coat. Bake for 30-40 minutes on each side or until wings are glazed and chicken juices run clear.

1 CHICKEN WING: 152 cal., 9g fat (3g sat. fat), 35mg chol., 107mg sod., 7g carb. (7g sugars, 0 fiber), 9g pro.

PEPPERMINT POPCORN

Crisp and minty, this simple snack is a hit with all 10 of our children. Feel free to use other candy flavors in place of the peppermint.
—Shirley Mars, Kent, OH

PREP: 10 min. • **MAKES:** 24 servings

- 1 lb. white candy coating, coarsely chopped
- 24 cups popped popcorn
- ½ to ¾ cup finely crushed peppermint candy (4 to 6 candy canes)
  Red nonpareils, optional

In a microwave, melt candy coating; stir until smooth. In a large bowl, combine the popcorn and crushed candy. Pour candy coating over top; toss to coat. Pour onto a waxed paper-lined baking sheet. If desired, sprinkle with nonpareils. When hardened, break apart. Store in an airtight container.

1 CUP: 163 cal., 8g fat (5g sat. fat), 0 chol., 98mg sod., 22g carb. (14g sugars, 1g fiber), 1g pro.

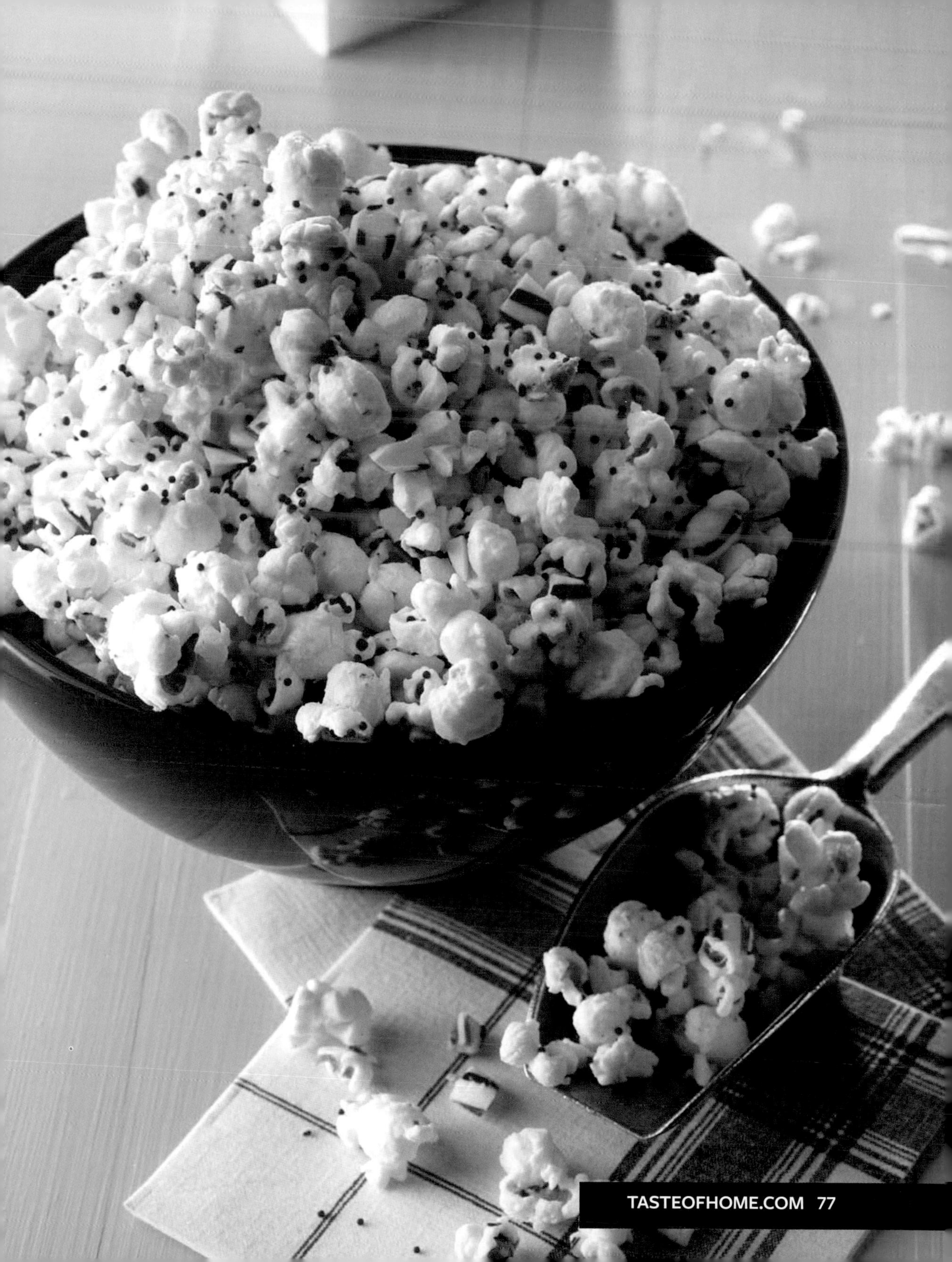

CHICKEN POT STICKERS

Chicken and mushrooms make up the filling in these pot stickers, which are traditional Chinese dumplings. Greasing the steamer rack makes it easy to remove them once they're steamed.
—Jacquelynne Stine, Las Vegas, NV

PREP: 50 min. • **COOK:** 5 min./batch • **MAKES:** 4 dozen

- 1 lb. boneless skinless chicken thighs, cut into chunks
- 1½ cups sliced fresh mushrooms
- 1 small onion, cut into wedges
- 2 Tbsp. hoisin sauce
- 2 Tbsp. prepared mustard
- 2 Tbsp. Sriracha chili sauce or 1 Tbsp. hot pepper sauce
- 1 pkg. (10 oz.) pot sticker or gyoza wrappers
- 1 large egg, lightly beaten

SAUCE
- 1 cup reduced-sodium soy sauce
- 1 green onion, chopped
- 1 tsp. ground ginger

1. In a food processor, combine the uncooked chicken, mushrooms, onion, hoisin sauce, mustard and chili sauce; cover and process until blended.
2. Place 1 Tbsp. chicken mixture in the center of 1 wrapper. (Until ready to use, keep remaining wrappers covered with a damp towel to prevent them from drying out.) Moisten entire edge with egg. Fold wrapper over filling to form a semicircle. Press edges firmly to seal, pleating the front side to form several folds.
3. Holding sealed edges, stand each dumpling on an even surface; press to flatten bottom. Curve ends to form a crescent shape. Repeat with remaining wrappers and filling.
4. Working in batches, arrange pot stickers in a single layer on a large greased steamer basket rack; place in a Dutch oven over 1 in. of water. Bring to a boil; cover and steam until filling juices run clear, 5-7 minutes. Repeat with remaining pot stickers.
5. Meanwhile, in a small bowl, combine sauce ingredients. Serve with pot stickers. Refrigerate leftovers.
FREEZE OPTION: Cover and freeze uncooked pot stickers in a single layer on waxed paper-lined sheets until firm. Transfer to resealable freezer containers; return to freezer. To use, steam as directed until heated through and juices run clear.
1 POT STICKER WITH 1 TSP. SAUCE: 43 cal., 1g fat (0 sat. fat), 11mg chol., 374mg sod., 5g carb. (0 sugars, 0 fiber), 3g pro.

INSPIRED BY:
PANDA EXPRESS'
CHICKEN POTSTICKER

DEEP-FRIED MAC & CHEESE SHELLS

I created this recipe for my husband, who loves mac and cheese. He describes this recipe as unbelievably delicious because of the crispy deep-fried coating and the creamy richness on the inside.
—Shirley Rickis, Lady Lake, FL

PREP: 45 min. • **COOK:** 15 min.
MAKES: 20 appetizers (2½ cups dipping sauce)

- 2 cups uncooked small pasta shells
- 20 uncooked jumbo pasta shells
- 2 Tbsp. butter
- 1 pkg. (16 oz.) process cheese (Velveeta), cubed
- 2 cups shredded cheddar cheese
- 1 cup heavy whipping cream
- ¾ cup grated Parmesan cheese, divided
- 1¼ cups 2% milk, divided
- 2 large eggs
- 2 cups panko (Japanese) bread crumbs
- ½ cup all-purpose flour
   Oil for deep-fat frying

1. Cook pastas separately according to package directions for al dente; drain. Meanwhile, in a large saucepan, melt butter over low heat. Add process cheese, cheddar cheese, cream and ¼ cup Parmesan cheese. Cook and stir over low heat until blended. Remove from heat.

2. In another large saucepan, combine small pasta shells and half of the cheese mixture; set aside. For dipping sauce, stir 1 cup milk into remaining cheese mixture; keep warm.

3. In a shallow bowl, whisk eggs with remaining milk. In another shallow bowl, mix bread crumbs with remaining Parmesan cheese. Place flour in a third shallow bowl. Fill each large shell with scant ¼ cup pasta mixture. Dip in flour to coat all sides; shake off excess. Dip in egg mixture, then in bread crumb mixture, patting to help coating adhere.

4. In an electric skillet or deep fryer, heat oil to 375°. Fry shells, a few at a time, 1-2 minutes on each side or until dark golden brown. Drain on paper towels. Serve with dipping sauce.

1 APPETIZER WITH 2 TBSP. DIPPING SAUCE: 340 cal., 23g fat (10g sat. fat), 72mg chol., 451mg sod., 21g carb. (3g sugars, 1g fiber), 12g pro.

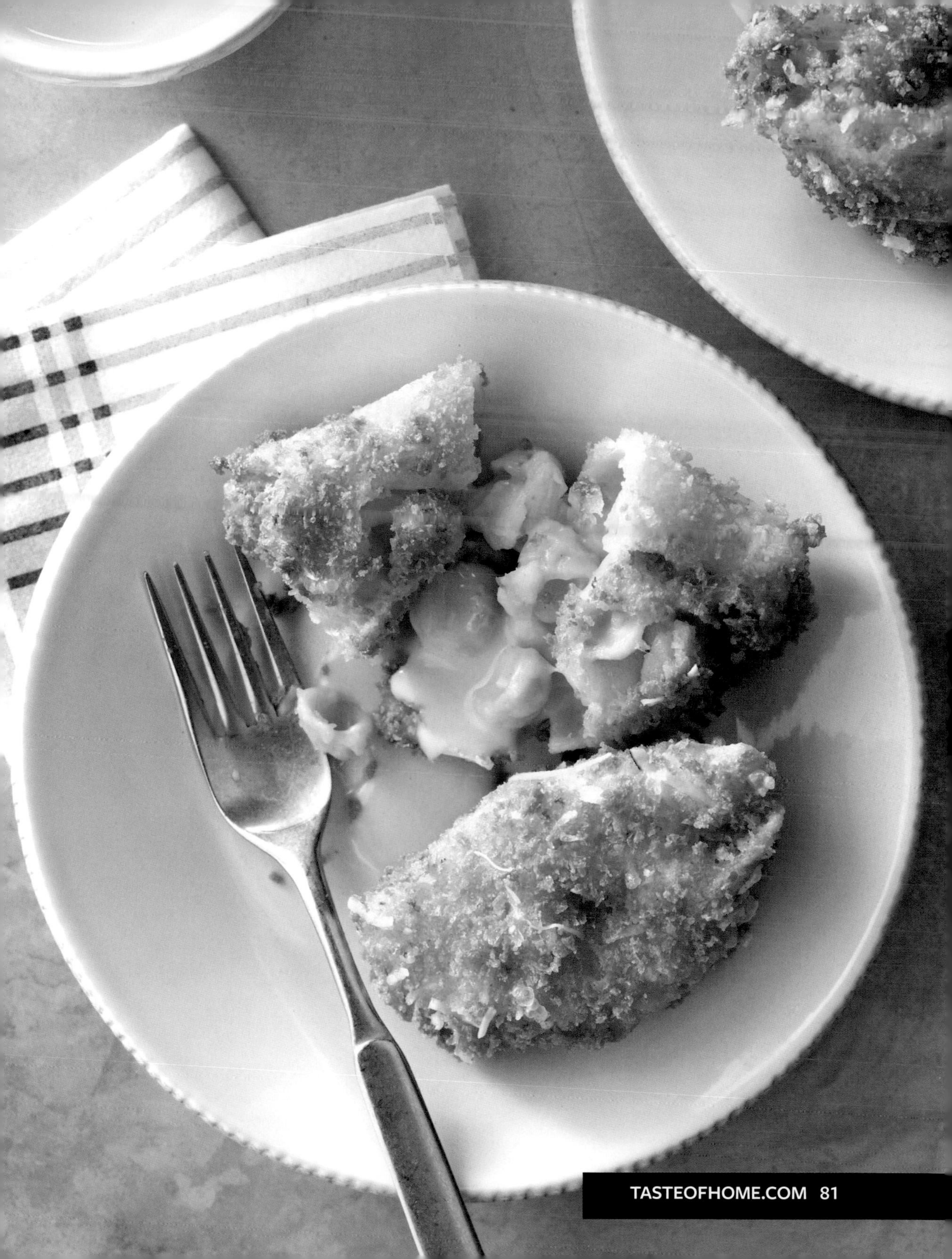

AVOCADO SALSA

I first served this salsa at a party, and it was a hit. People love the garlic, corn and avocado combination.
—Susan Vandermeer, Ogden, UT

PREP: 20 min. + chilling • **MAKES:** about 7 cups

- 1⅔ cups (about 8¼ oz.) frozen corn, thawed
- 2 cans (2¼ oz. each) sliced ripe olives, drained
- 1 medium sweet red pepper, chopped
- 1 small onion, chopped
- 5 garlic cloves, minced
- ⅓ cup olive oil
- ¼ cup lemon juice
- 3 Tbsp. cider vinegar
- 1 tsp. dried oregano
- ½ tsp. salt
- ½ tsp. pepper
- 4 medium ripe avocados, peeled
  Tortilla chips

1. Combine corn, olives, red pepper and onion. In another bowl, mix the next 7 ingredients. Pour over corn mixture; toss to coat. Refrigerate, covered, overnight.

2. Just before serving, chop avocados; stir into salsa. Serve with tortilla chips.

¼ CUP: 82 cal., 7g fat (1g sat. fat), 0 chol., 85mg sod., 5g carb. (1g sugars, 2g fiber), 1g pro.
DIABETIC EXCHANGES: 1½ fat.

CHICKEN FRIES

These crunchy and kid-friendly oven-baked chicken fries are coated with a mixture of crushed potato chips, panko bread crumbs and Parmesan cheese. Dip them in ranch dressing, barbecue sauce or honey-mustard sauce.
—Nick Iverson, Denver, CO

PREP: 20 min. • **BAKE:** 15 min. • **MAKES:** 4 servings

- 2 **large eggs, lightly beaten**
- ½ **tsp. salt**
- ½ **tsp. garlic powder**
- ¼ **to ½ tsp. cayenne pepper**
- 2 **cups finely crushed ridged potato chips**
- 1 **cup panko (Japanese) bread crumbs**
- ½ **cup grated Parmesan cheese**
- 2 **boneless skinless chicken breasts (6 oz. each), cut into ¼-in.-thick strips**

Preheat oven to 400°. In a shallow bowl, whisk eggs, salt, garlic powder and cayenne. In a separate shallow bowl, combine chips, bread crumbs and cheese. Dip chicken in egg mixture, then in potato chip mixture, patting to help coating adhere. Transfer to a greased wire rack in a foil-lined rimmed baking sheet. Bake until golden brown, 12-15 minutes.

1 SERVING: 376 cal., 17g fat (6g sat. fat), 149mg chol., 761mg sod., 27g carb. (1g sugars, 2g fiber), 27g pro.

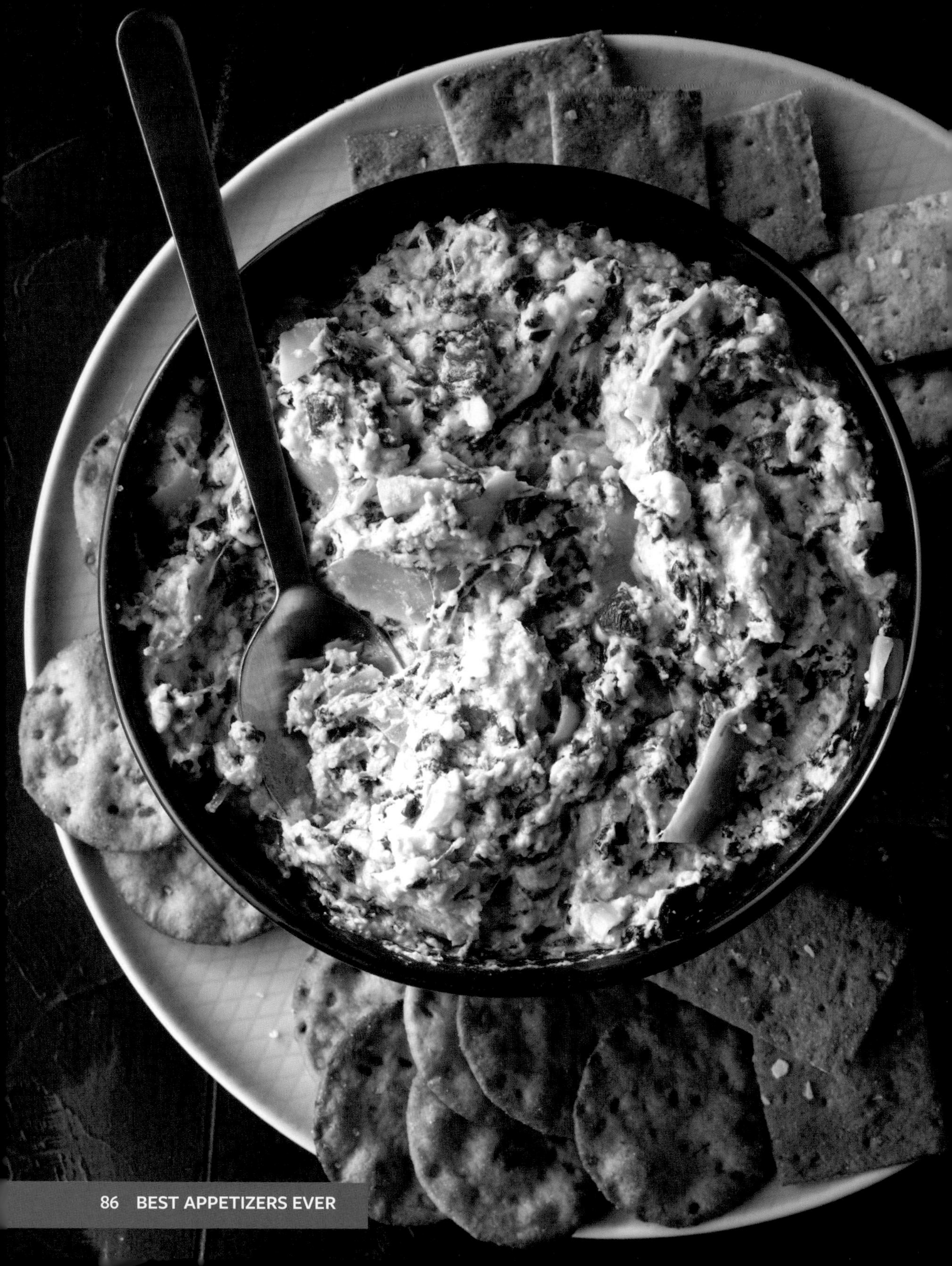

FIVE-CHEESE SPINACH & ARTICHOKE DIP

Here is the recipe that I am always asked to bring to events. I make it for weddings, Christmas parties and more. This dip can also be baked in an oven at about 400 degrees for 30 minutes or until hot and bubbly.
—Noelle Myers, Grand Forks, ND

PREP: 20 min. • **COOK:** 2½ hours • **MAKES:** 16 servings

- 1 jar (12 oz.) roasted sweet red peppers
- 1 jar (6½ oz.) marinated quartered artichoke hearts
- 1 pkg. (10 oz.) frozen chopped spinach, thawed and squeezed dry
- 8 oz. fresh mozzarella cheese, cubed
- 1½ cups shredded Asiago cheese
- 6 oz. cream cheese, softened and cubed
- 1 cup crumbled feta cheese
- ⅓ cup shredded provolone cheese
- ⅓ cup minced fresh basil
- ¼ cup finely chopped red onion
- 2 Tbsp. mayonnaise
- 2 garlic cloves, minced
  Assorted crackers

1. Drain peppers, reserving 1 Tbsp. liquid; chop peppers. Drain artichokes, reserving 2 Tbsp. liquid; coarsely chop artichokes.
2. In a 3-qt. slow cooker coated with cooking spray, combine spinach, cheeses, basil, onion, mayonnaise, garlic, artichoke hearts and peppers. Stir in reserved pepper and artichoke liquids. Cook, covered, on high 2 hours. Stir dip; cook, covered, until cheese is melted, 30-60 minutes longer. Stir before serving; serve with crackers.

¼ CUP: 197 cal., 16g fat (8g sat. fat), 38mg chol., 357mg sod., 4g carb. (2g sugars, 1g fiber), 9g pro.

SWEET & SPICY ASIAN MEATBALLS

For my niece's annual Halloween party, I make sweet and spicy meatballs. I bring them in the slow cooker so they're ready to eat.
—Gail Borczyk, Boca Raton, FL

PREP: 1 hour • **COOK:** 3 hours • **MAKES:** about 5 dozen

- 1 large egg, lightly beaten
- ½ medium onion, finely chopped
- ⅓ cup sliced water chestnuts, minced
- 3 Tbsp. minced fresh cilantro
- 1 jalapeno pepper, seeded and finely chopped
- 3 Tbsp. reduced-sodium soy sauce
- 4 garlic cloves, minced
- 1 Tbsp. minced fresh gingerroot
- ⅔ cup panko (Japanese) bread crumbs
- 2 lbs. ground pork

SAUCE
- 2 cups sweet-and-sour sauce
- ¼ cup barbecue sauce
- ¼ cup duck sauce
- 2 Tbsp. chicken broth
- 1 Tbsp. minced fresh cilantro
- 1 Tbsp. reduced-sodium soy sauce
- 2 garlic cloves, minced
- 1½ tsp. minced fresh gingerroot
    Thinly sliced green onions, optional

1. Preheat oven to 375°. In a large bowl, combine first 8 ingredients; stir in bread crumbs. Add the pork; mix lightly but thoroughly. Shape into 1¼-in. balls. Place meatballs on a greased rack in a 15x10x1-in. baking pan. Bake 18-22 minutes or until lightly browned.
2. Transfer meatballs to a 4-qt. slow cooker. In small bowl, mix the first 8 sauce ingredients. Pour over meatballs. Cook, covered, on low 3-4 hours or until meatballs are cooked through. If desired, sprinkle with green onions.
FREEZE OPTION: Freeze cooled meatball mixture in freezer containers. To use, partially thaw in refrigerator overnight. Heat through in a covered saucepan, gently stirring and adding a little broth or water if necessary. Sprinkle with green onions if desired.
NOTE: Wear disposable gloves when cutting hot peppers; the oils can burn skin. Avoid touching your face.
1 MEATBALL: 52 cal., 2g fat (1g sat. fat), 13mg chol., 119mg sod., 4g carb. (3g sugars, 0 fiber), 3g pro.

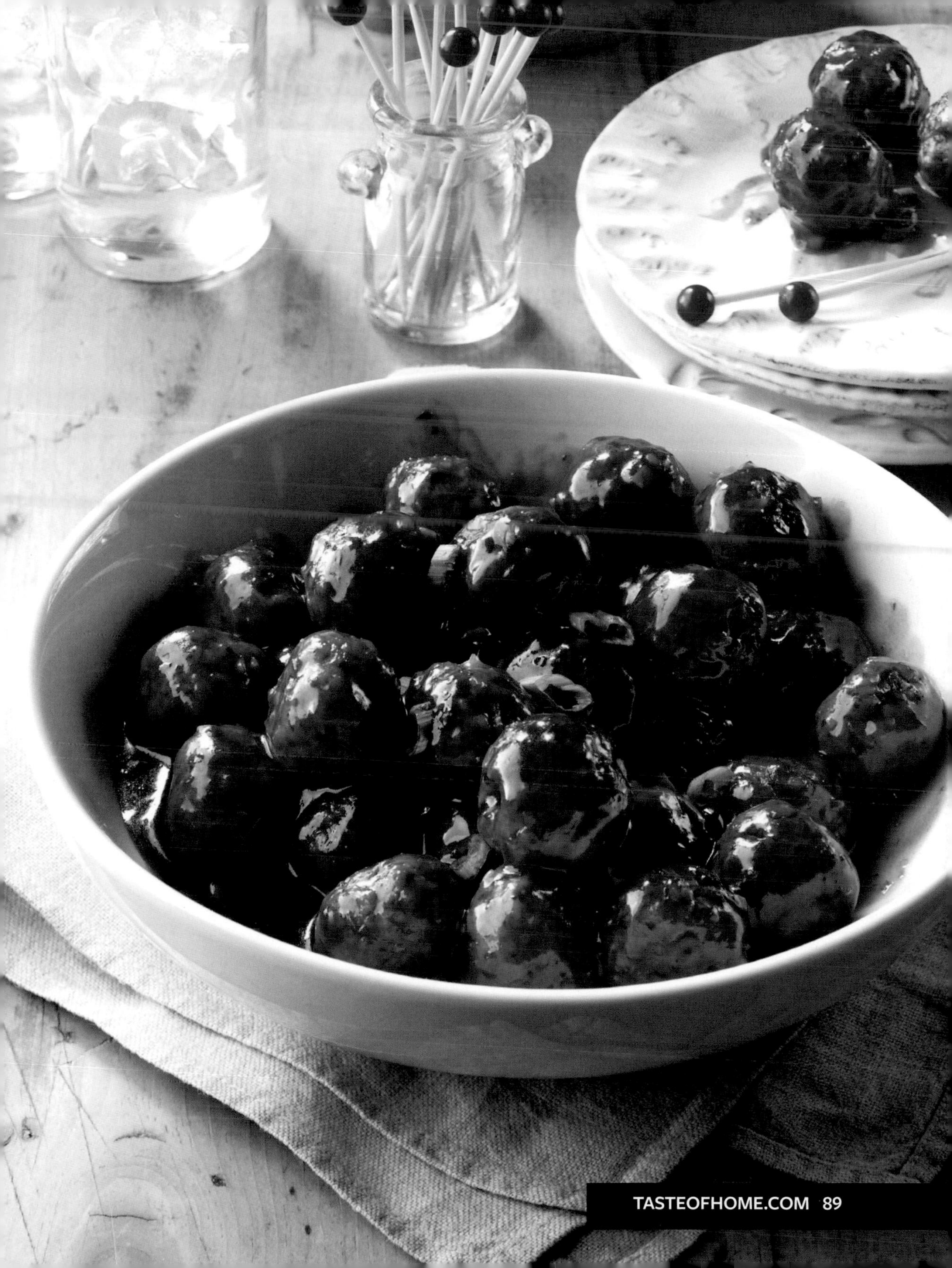

INSPIRED BY:
BUFFALO WILD WINGS'
HONEY BBQ WINGS

GLAZED CHICKEN WINGS

I received the recipe for these yummy wings from a cousin while visiting her on Vancouver Island. They're an appealing appetizer, but also make a great lunch or dinner when served with hot rice and a salad.
—Joan Airey, Rivers, MB

PREP: 15 min. • **BAKE:** 50 min. • **MAKES:** 2 dozen

2½ lbs. chicken wings
½ cup barbecue sauce
½ cup honey
½ cup soy sauce

Cut chicken wings into 3 sections; discard wing tip section. Place in a greased 13x9-in. baking dish. Combine barbecue sauce, honey and soy sauce; pour over wings. Bake, uncovered, at 350° for 50-60 minutes or until chicken juices run clear.

NOTE: Uncooked chicken wing sections (wingettes) may be substituted for whole chicken wings.

1 CHICKEN WING: 86 cal., 4g fat (1g sat. fat), 15mg chol., 380mg sod., 8g carb. (8g sugars, 0 fiber), 6g pro.

SOUTHERN FRIED OKRA

Golden brown with a little fresh green popping through, these okra nuggets are crunchy and addicting! My sons like to dip them in ketchup.
—Pam Duncan, Summers, AR

TAKES: 30 min. • **MAKES:** 2 servings

1½ cups sliced fresh or frozen okra, thawed
3 Tbsp. buttermilk
2 Tbsp. all-purpose flour
2 Tbsp. cornmeal
¼ tsp. salt
¼ tsp. garlic herb seasoning blend
⅛ tsp. pepper
   Oil for deep-fat frying
   Additional salt and pepper, optional

1. Pat okra dry with paper towels. Place the buttermilk in a shallow bowl. In another shallow bowl, combine the flour, cornmeal, salt, seasoning blend and pepper. Dip okra in buttermilk, then roll in cornmeal mixture.
2. In an electric skillet or deep-fat fryer, heat 1 in. of oil to 375°. Fry okra, a few pieces at a time, for 1½-2½ minutes on each side or until golden brown. Drain on paper towels. Season with additional salt and pepper if desired.
¾ CUP: 368 cal., 31g fat (2g sat. fat), 1mg chol., 410mg sod., 19g carb. (4g sugars, 4g fiber), 5g pro.

INSPIRED BY:
CRACKER BARREL'S BREADED FRIED OKRA

TATER TOT-CHOS

Playing with food is loads of fun when you have Tater Tots and taco toppings. Let kids build their own for smiles all around.
—Eleanor Mielke, Mitchell, SD

TAKES: 30 min. • **MAKES:** 6 servings

- 4 **cups frozen miniature Tater Tots**
- 1 **lb. ground beef**
- 1 **envelope reduced-sodium taco seasoning**
- ⅔ **cup water**
- ½ **cup shredded cheddar cheese**
- 2 **cups shredded lettuce**
- ¼ **cup sliced ripe olives, optional**
- ¼ **cup taco sauce**
- ½ **cup sour cream**

1. Bake Tater Tots according to package directions.
2. Meanwhile, in a large skillet, cook beef over medium heat until no longer pink, breaking into crumbles, 6-8 minutes; drain. Stir in taco seasoning and water. Bring to a boil; cook and stir until thickened, about 2 minutes.
3. To serve, top Tater Tots with beef mixture, cheese, lettuce and, if desired, olives. Serve with taco sauce and sour cream.

1 SERVING: 375 cal., 23g fat (9g sat. fat), 70mg chol., 828mg sod., 27g carb. (4g sugars, 2g fiber), 18g pro.

BAKED EGG ROLLS

These baked beauties are low in fat, but their crisp baked texture will fool you into thinking they're fried! Serve with your favorite Asian dipping sauce.

—Barbara Lierman, Lyons, NE

PREP: 30 min. • **BAKE:** 10 min. • **MAKES:** 8 servings

- 2 cups grated carrots
- 1 can (14 oz.) bean sprouts, drained
- ½ cup chopped water chestnuts
- ¼ cup chopped green pepper
- ¼ cup chopped green onions
- 1 garlic clove, minced
- 2 cups finely diced cooked chicken
- 4 tsp. cornstarch
- 1 Tbsp. water
- 1 Tbsp. light soy sauce
- 1 tsp. canola oil
- 1 tsp. brown sugar
  Pinch cayenne pepper
- 16 egg roll wrappers
  Cooking spray

1. Coat a large skillet with cooking spray; add the first 6 ingredients. Cook and stir over medium heat until vegetables are crisp-tender, about 3 minutes. Add chicken; heat through.

2. In a small bowl, combine the cornstarch, water, soy sauce, oil, brown sugar and cayenne until smooth; stir into chicken mixture. Bring to a boil. Cook and stir for 2 minutes or until thickened; remove from the heat.

3. Spoon ¼ cup chicken mixture on the bottom third of 1 egg roll wrapper; fold sides toward center and roll tightly. (Keep remaining wrappers covered with a damp paper towel until ready to use.) Place seam side down on a baking sheet coated with cooking spray. Repeat.

4. Spritz tops of egg rolls with cooking spray. Bake at 425° for 10-15 minutes or until lightly browned.

FREEZE OPTION: Freeze cooled egg rolls in a freezer container, separating layers with waxed paper. To use, reheat rolls on a baking sheet in a preheated 350° oven until crisp and heated through.

2 EGG ROLLS: 261 cal., 3g fat (0 sat. fat), 27mg chol., 518mg sod., 45g carb. (0 sugars, 0 fiber), 13g pro.

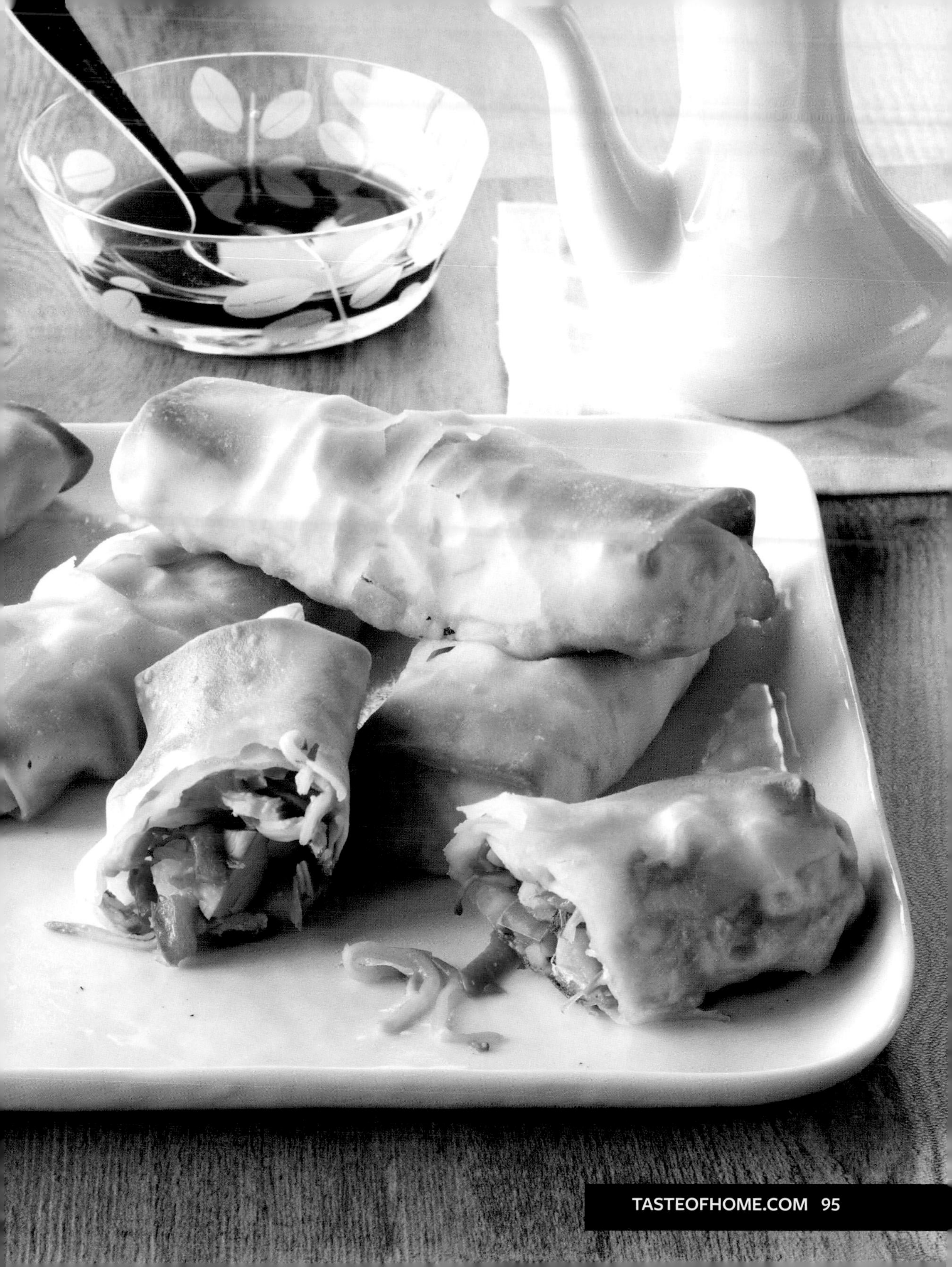

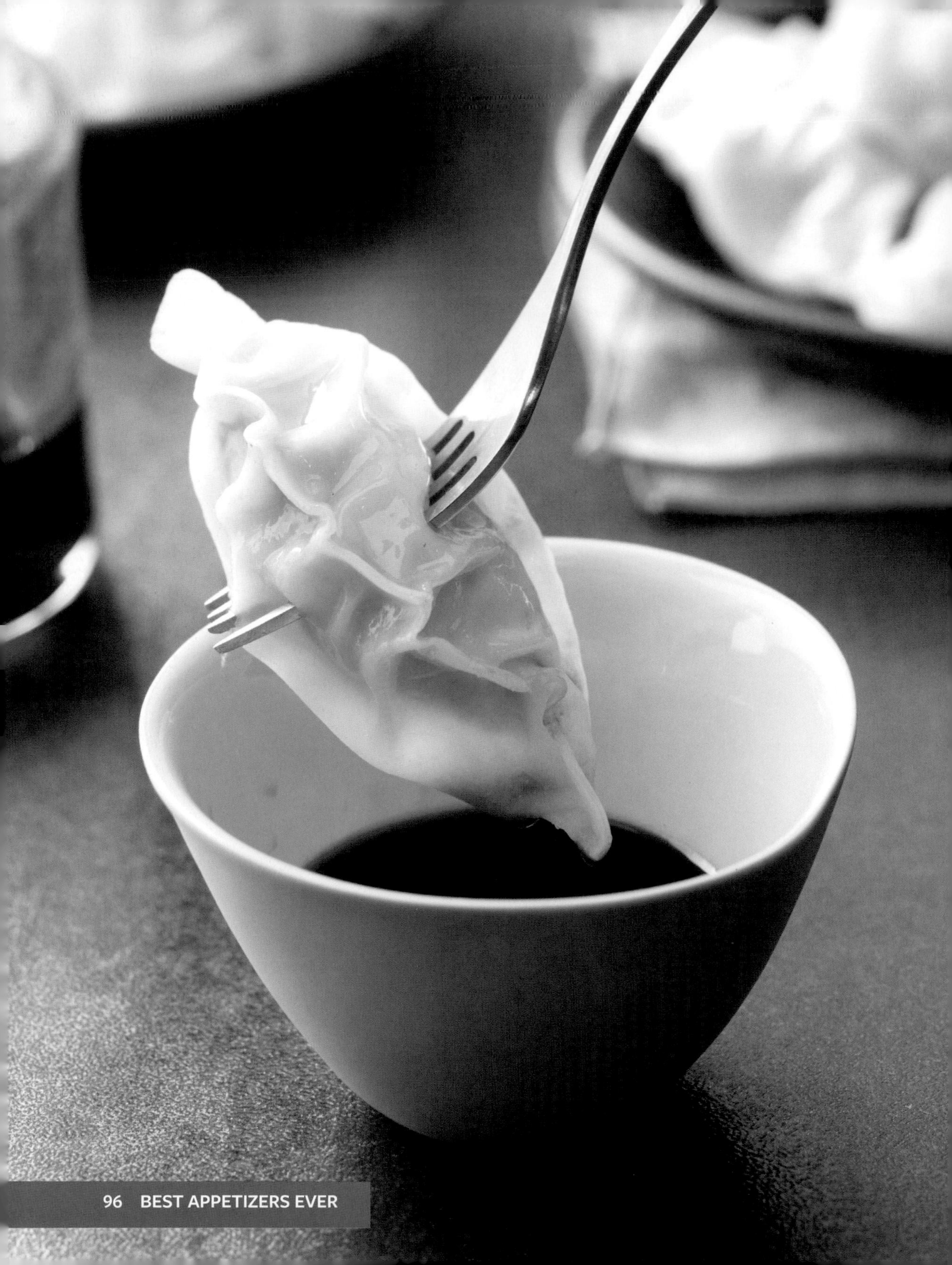

ASIAN CHICKEN DUMPLINGS

We occasionally make Chinese food to celebrate our daughters' heritage, especially around holidays like the Lunar New Year. I took a traditional pork dumpling recipe and modified it to use ground chicken. Feel free to sprinkle cilantro, sesame seeds or scallions on top for extra flair.
—Joy Olcott, Millersville, PA

PREP: 40 min. • **COOK:** 10 min./batch • **MAKES:** 2½ dozen

- 1   lb. ground chicken
- 4   green onions, chopped
- ½   cup chopped cabbage
- ¼   cup minced fresh cilantro
- 2   tsp. minced fresh gingerroot
- 1   tsp. salt
- ¼   tsp. Chinese five-spice powder
- 2   Tbsp. water
- 1   pkg. (10 oz.) pot sticker or gyoza wrappers
     Cabbage leaves
     Reduced-sodium soy sauce

1. Place first 7 ingredients in a food processor; cover and process until finely chopped. Add water; cover and process until blended.
2. Place 1 Tbsp. chicken mixture in the center of 1 wrapper. (Keep remaining wrappers covered with a damp paper towel to prevent them from drying out.) Moisten edges with water. Fold wrapper over filling to form a semicircle; press edges firmly to seal, pleating the front side to form 3 to 5 folds.
3. Holding sealed edges, stand each dumpling on an even surface; press to flatten bottom. Repeat with remaining wrappers and filling; cover dumplings with plastic wrap.
4. Line a steamer basket with 4 cabbage leaves. Arrange the dumplings in batches 1 in. apart over cabbage; place in a large saucepan over 1 in. of water. Bring to a boil; cover and steam for 10-12 minutes or until a thermometer reads 165°. Discard cabbage. Repeat. Serve with soy sauce.
1 DUMPLING: 45 cal., 1g fat (0 sat. fat), 10mg chol., 109mg sod., 6g carb. (0 sugars, 0 fiber), 3g pro.

INSPIRED BY:
CALIFORNIA PIZZA KITCHEN'S SZECHWAN CHICKEN DUMPLINGS

INSPIRED BY:
RED ROBIN'S
FRIED PICKLE NICKELS

OVEN-FRIED PICKLES

LIke deep-fried pickles? You'll love this unfried version even more. Dill pickle spears are coated with panko bread crumbs and spices, then baked until crispy. Dip them in ranch salad dressing for an unforgettable appetizer.
—Nick Iverson, Denver, CO

PREP: 20 min. + standing • **BAKE:** 20 min. • **MAKES:** 8 servings

- 32 dill pickle slices
- ½ cup all-purpose flour
- ½ tsp. salt
- 2 large eggs, lightly beaten
- 2 Tbsp. dill pickle juice
- ½ tsp. cayenne pepper
- ½ tsp. garlic powder
- ½ cup panko (Japanese) bread crumbs
- 1 Tbsp. snipped fresh dill

1. Preheat oven to 500°. Let pickles stand on a paper towel until liquid is almost absorbed, about 15 minutes.
2. Meanwhile, in a shallow bowl, combine flour and salt. In another shallow bowl, whisk eggs, pickle juice, cayenne and garlic powder. Combine panko and dill in a third shallow bowl.
3. Dip pickles in flour mixture to coat both sides; shake off excess. Dip in egg mixture, then in crumb mixture, patting to help coating adhere. Transfer to a greased wire rack in a rimmed baking sheet.
4. Bake until golden brown and crispy, 20-25 minutes.
4 PICKLE SLICES: 65 cal., 2g fat (0 sat. fat), 47mg chol., 421mg sod., 9g carb. (1g sugars, 1g fiber), 3g pro.

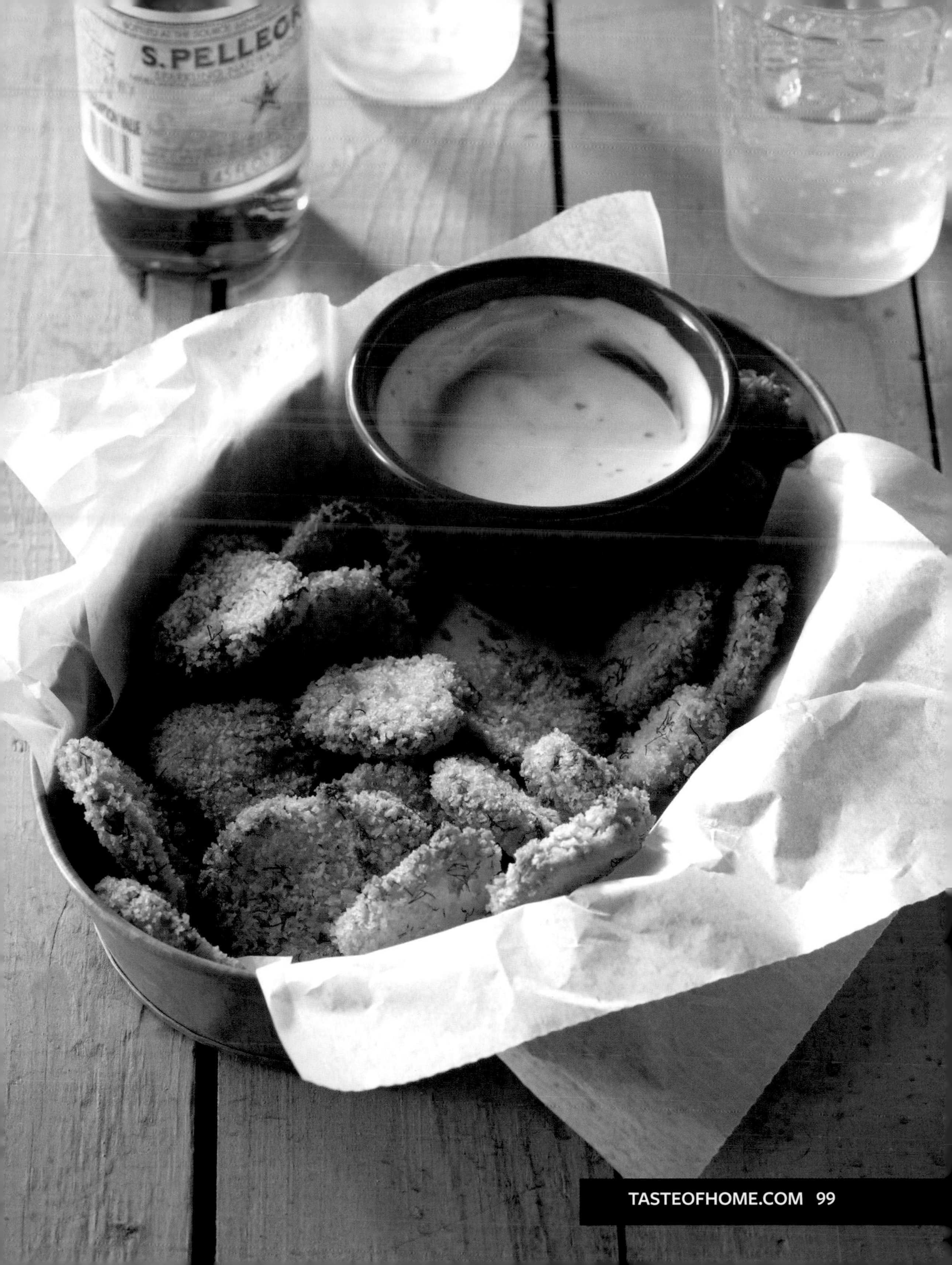

INSPIRED BY:
ROCK BOTTOM RESTAURANT
& BREWERY'S
BACON JALAPENO POPPERS

SWEET & SPICY JALAPENO POPPERS

There's no faster—or tastier!— way to get a party started than with these bacon-wrapped poppers. Assemble them in advance and bake just before serving.
—Dawn Onuffer, Crestview, FL

TAKES: 30 min. • **MAKES:** 1 dozen

- 6 jalapeno peppers
- 4 oz. cream cheese, softened
- 2 Tbsp. shredded cheddar cheese
- 6 bacon strips, halved widthwise
- ¼ cup packed brown sugar
- 1 Tbsp. chili seasoning mix

1. Cut jalapenos in half lengthwise and remove seeds; set aside. In a small bowl, beat cheeses until blended. Spoon into pepper halves. Wrap a half-strip of bacon around each pepper half.
2. Combine brown sugar and chili seasoning; coat peppers with sugar mixture. Place in a greased 15x10x1-in. baking pan.
3. Bake at 350° until bacon is firm, 18-20 minutes.
NOTE: Wear disposable gloves when cutting hot peppers; the oils can burn skin. Avoid touching your face.
1 STUFFED PEPPER HALF: 66 cal., 5g fat (3g sat. fat), 15mg chol., 115mg sod., 3g carb. (3g sugars, 0 fiber), 2g pro.

ITALIAN SAUSAGE BRUSCHETTA

Sometimes I garnish each slice of this bruschetta with a sprig of fresh basil. It's a classic appetizer everyone loves.
—Teresa Ralston, New Albany, OH

TAKES: 20 min. • **MAKES:** 2 dozen

- 1 lb. bulk Italian sausage
- 8 oz. mascarpone cheese, softened
- 3 Tbsp. prepared pesto
- 24 slices French bread baguette (½ in. thick)
- 3 Tbsp. olive oil
- ¾ cup finely chopped seeded plum tomatoes
- 3 Tbsp. chopped fresh parsley
- 3 Tbsp. shredded Parmesan cheese

1. In a large skillet, cook sausage over medium heat 6-8 minutes or until no longer pink, breaking into crumbles; drain. In a small bowl, combine mascarpone cheese and pesto.

2. Preheat broiler. Place bread on ungreased baking sheets. Brush bread slices on 1 side with oil. Broil 3-4 in. from the heat until golden brown, 30-45 seconds on each side. Spread with mascarpone mixture. Top each with sausage, tomatoes, parsley and Parmesan cheese. Serve warm.

1 APPETIZER: 131 cal., 11g fat (4g sat. fat), 22mg chol., 202mg sod., 5g carb. (0 sugars, 0 fiber), 4g pro.

Specialty Soups, Salads & Sandwiches

EAT THEM ON THEIR OWN, OR PAIR 'EM UP—THE RECIPES IN THIS CHAPTER LET YOU MIX AND MATCH SOUPS, SALADS AND SANDWICHES FROM YOUR FAVORITE RESTAURANTS!

BACON & SWISS
CHICKEN SANDWICHES, P. 129
INSPIRED BY: APPLEBEE'S
BACON CHEDDAR
GRILLED CHICKEN SANDWICH

INSPIRED BY:
WENDY'S
TACO SALAD

GROUND BEEF TACO SALAD

Everyone at our house loves this zesty taco salad. In spring, we enjoy light and refreshing entrees like this, especially after the heavier comfort foods of winter.
—Muriel Bertrand, Shoreview, MN

TAKES: 25 min. • **MAKES:** 2 servings

- ½ lb. ground beef
- ⅓ cup bean dip
- 1 tsp. chili powder
- ¼ tsp. salt
- 1 cup canned diced tomatoes plus 2 Tbsp. liquid
- 2 cups chopped lettuce
- ½ cup shredded cheddar cheese
- 2 green onions, sliced
- 2 Tbsp. sliced ripe olives
- ½ cup corn chips

1. In a large skillet, cook ground beef over medium heat until no longer pink; drain. Stir in the bean dip, chili powder, salt and tomato liquid. Remove from the heat.
2. In a large bowl, combine the diced tomatoes, lettuce, cheese, onions and olives. Add beef mixture; toss to coat. Top with chips. Serve immediately.
2 CUPS: 469 cal., 28g fat (12g sat. fat), 107mg chol., 1007mg sod., 25g carb. (5g sugars, 4g fiber), 32g pro.

COPYCAT CHICKEN SALAD

This chicken salad sandwich tastes incredibly close to the real thing from Chick-fil-A. Your family will love it! The sweet pickle relish gives it a distinctive taste. I use a thick crusty oat bread, but use any you like.
—Julie Peterson, Crofton, MD

TAKES: 20 min. • **MAKES:** 2 servings

- ½ cup reduced-fat mayonnaise
- ⅓ cup sweet pickle relish
- ⅓ cup finely chopped celery
- ½ tsp. sugar
- ¼ tsp. salt
- ¼ tsp. pepper
- 1 hard-boiled large egg, cooled and minced
- 2 cups chopped cooked chicken breast
- 4 slices whole wheat bread, toasted
- 2 romaine leaves

Mix the first 7 ingredients; stir in chicken. Line 2 slices of toast with lettuce. Top with chicken salad and remaining toast.

1 SANDWICH: 651 cal., 29g fat (5g sat. fat), 222mg chol., 1386mg sod., 45g carb. (18g sugars, 4g fiber), 51g pro.

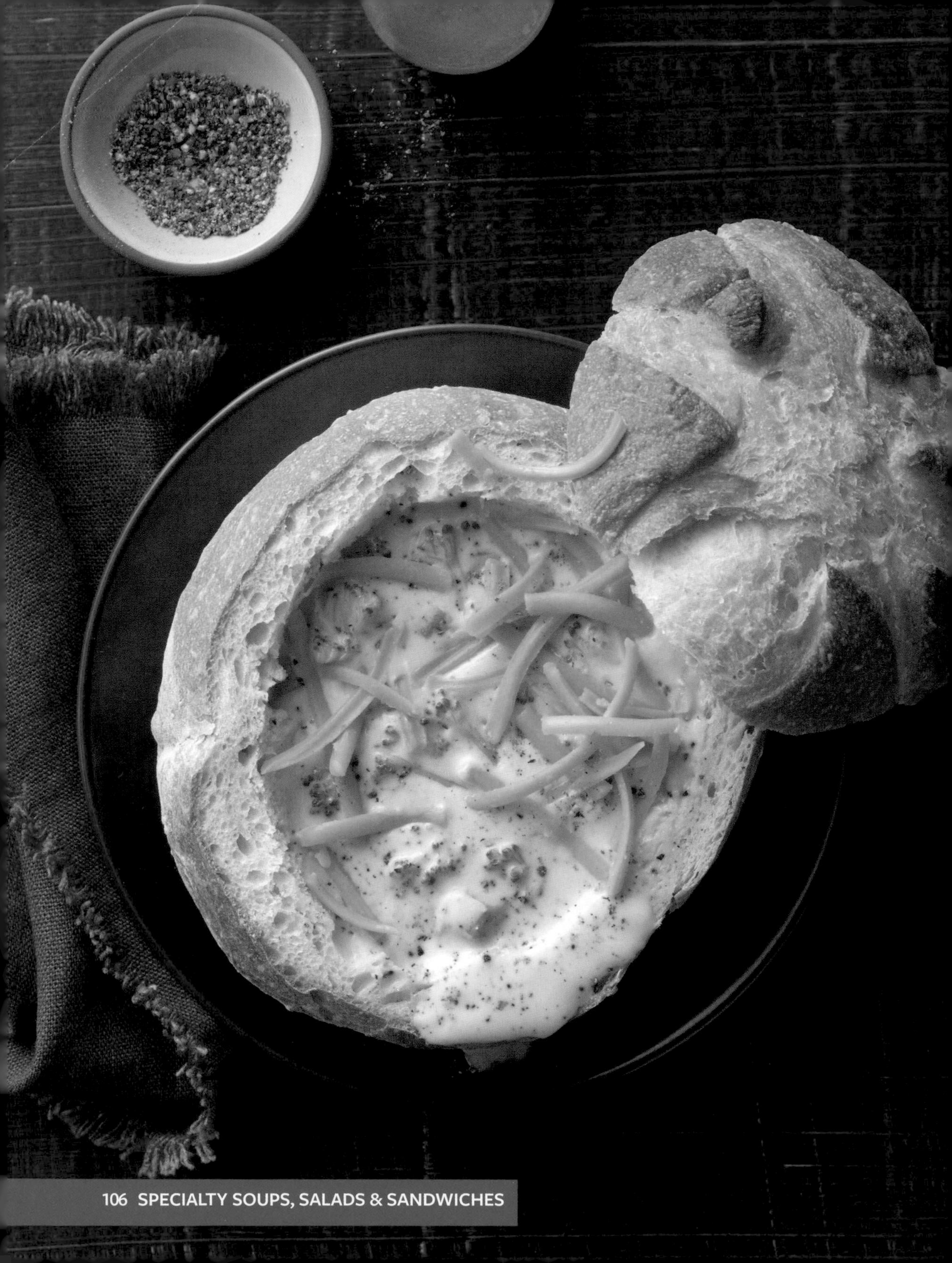

CHEESY BROCCOLI SOUP IN A BREAD BOWL

This creamy, cheesy broccoli soup tastes just like the kind served at Panera. My family requests it all the time. You can even make your own homemade bread bowls with the recipe on my blog, Yammie's Noshery.
—Rachel Preus, Marshall, MI

PREP: 15 min. • **COOK:** 30 min. • **MAKES:** 6 servings

- ¼ cup butter, cubed
- ½ cup chopped onion
- 2 garlic cloves, minced
- 4 cups fresh broccoli florets (about 8 oz.)
- 1 large carrot, finely chopped
- 3 cups chicken stock
- 2 cups half-and-half cream
- 2 bay leaves
- ½ tsp. salt
- ¼ tsp. ground nutmeg
- ¼ tsp. pepper
- ¼ cup cornstarch
- ¼ cup water or additional chicken stock
- 2½ cups shredded cheddar cheese
- 6 small round bread loaves (about 8 oz. each), optional

1. In a 6-qt. stockpot, heat butter over medium heat; saute onion and garlic until tender, 6-8 minutes. Stir in broccoli, carrot, stock, cream and seasonings; bring to a boil. Simmer, uncovered, until vegetables are tender, 10-12 minutes.

2. Mix cornstarch and water until smooth; stir into soup. Bring to a boil, stirring occasionally; cook and stir until thickened, 1-2 minutes. Remove bay leaves. Stir in cheese until melted.

3. If using bread bowls, cut a slice off the top of each bread loaf; hollow out bottoms, leaving ¼-in.-thick shells (save removed bread for another use). Fill with soup just before serving.

1 CUP: 422 cal., 32g fat (19g sat. fat), 107mg chol., 904mg sod., 15g carb. (5g sugars, 2g fiber), 17g pro.

INSPIRED BY:
PANERA BREAD'S BROCCOLI CHEDDAR SOUP

HAVE IT YOUR WAY

Avoid a gritty cheese soup by allowing the liquid mixture to cool slightly before adding the shredded cheese. Stir in a little at a time until all the cheese is melted.

STRAWBERRY SALAD WITH POPPY SEED DRESSING

My family is always happy to see this fruit and veggie salad on the table. If fresh strawberries aren't available, substitute mandarin oranges and dried cranberries.

—Irene Keller, Kalamazoo, MI

TAKES: 30 min. • **MAKES:** 10 servings

¼ cup sugar
⅓ cup slivered almonds
1 bunch romaine, torn (about 8 cups)
1 small onion, halved and thinly sliced
2 cups halved fresh strawberries

DRESSING

¼ cup mayonnaise
2 Tbsp. sugar
1 Tbsp. sour cream
1 Tbsp. 2% milk
2¼ tsp. cider vinegar
1½ tsp. poppy seeds

1. Place sugar in a small heavy skillet; cook and stir over medium-low heat until melted and caramel-colored, about 10 minutes. Stir in almonds until coated. Spread on foil to cool.

2. Place romaine, onion and strawberries in a large bowl. Whisk together dressing ingredients; toss with salad. Break candied almonds into pieces; sprinkle over salad. Serve immediately.

¾ CUP: 110 cal., 6g fat (1g sat. fat), 1mg chol., 33mg sod., 13g carb. (10g sugars, 2g fiber), 2g pro.

DIABETIC EXCHANGES: ½ starch, 1 vegetable, 1 fat.

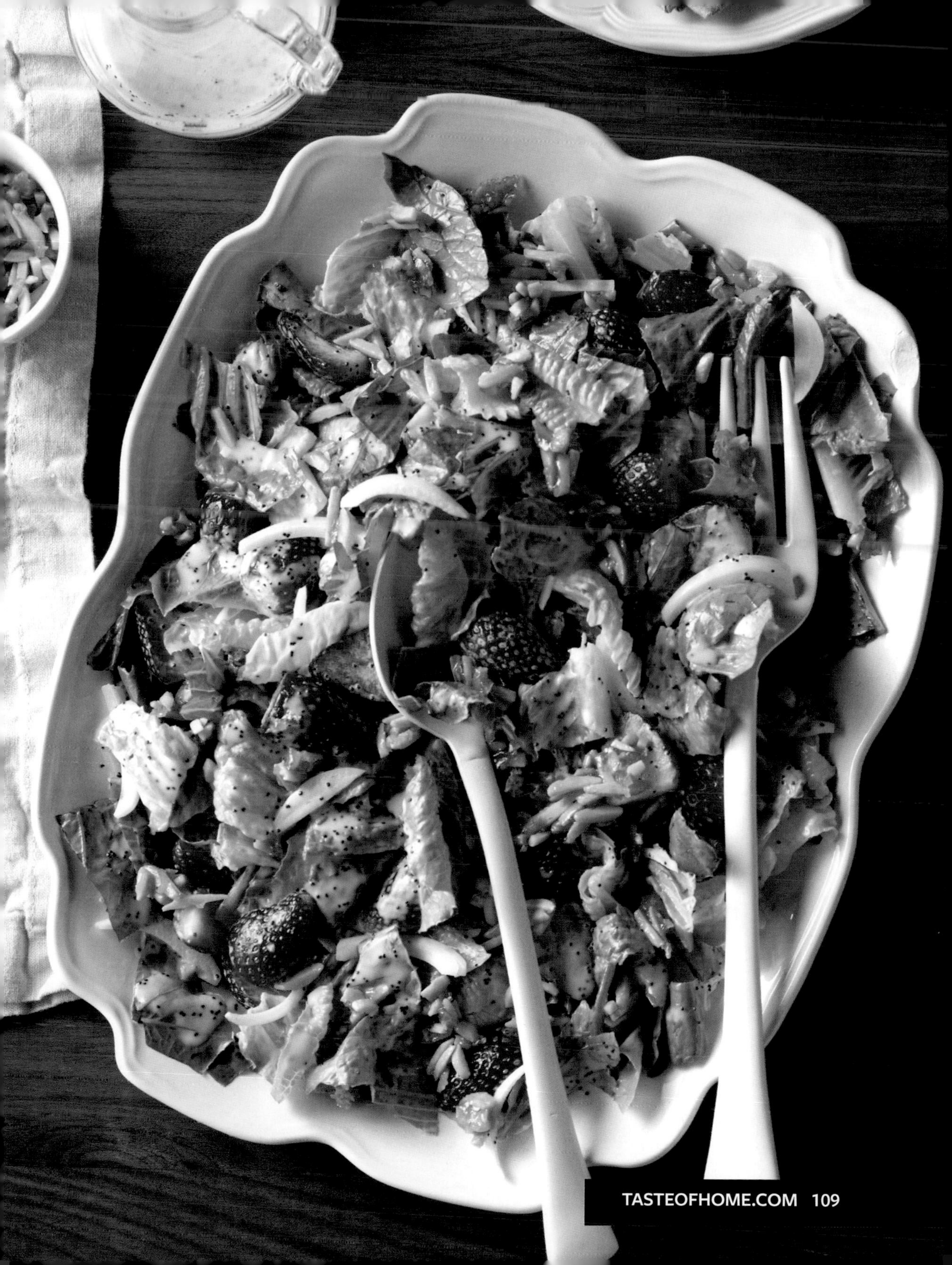

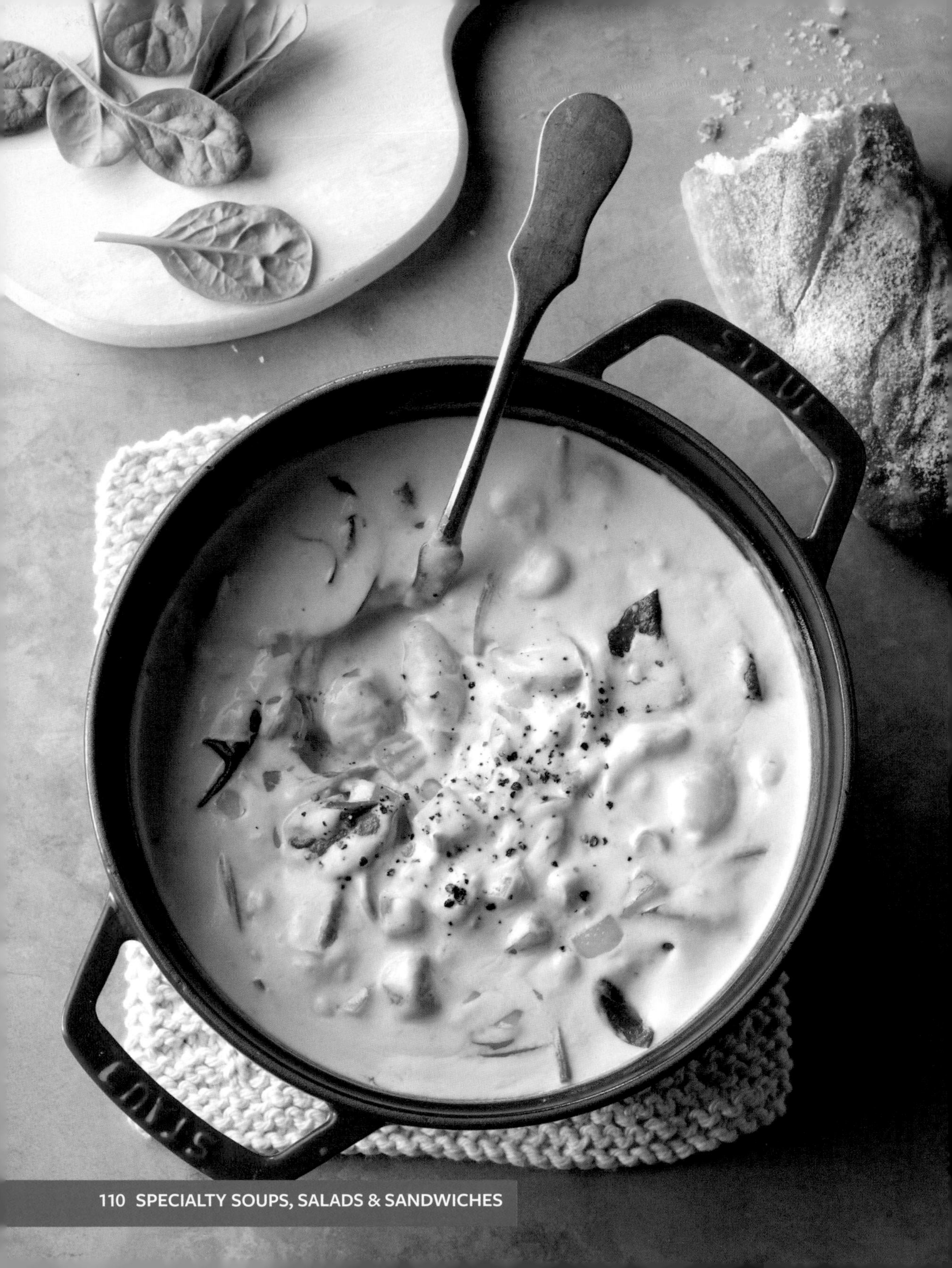
STAUB
STAUB

CREAMY CHICKEN GNOCCHI SOUP

I tasted a similar soup at Olive Garden and wanted to make it myself. Here's the delicious result! It's wonderful on a cool evening.
—Jaclynn Robinson, Shingletown, CA

INSPIRED BY:
OLIVE GARDEN'S
CHICKEN & GNOCCHI SOUP

PREP: 25 min. • **COOK:** 15 min. • **MAKES:** 8 servings (2 qt.)

- 1 lb. boneless skinless chicken breasts, cut into ½-in. pieces
- ⅓ cup butter, divided
- 1 small onion, chopped
- 1 medium carrot, shredded
- 1 celery rib, chopped
- 2 garlic cloves, minced
- ⅓ cup all-purpose flour
- 3½ cups 2% milk
- 1½ cups heavy whipping cream
- 1 Tbsp. reduced-sodium chicken bouillon granules
- ¼ tsp. coarsely ground pepper
- 1 pkg. (16 oz.) potato gnocchi
- ½ cup chopped fresh spinach

1. In a Dutch oven, brown chicken in 2 Tbsp. butter. Remove and keep warm. In the same pan, saute the onion, carrot, celery and garlic in remaining butter until tender.

2. Whisk in flour until blended; gradually stir in the milk, cream, bouillon and pepper. Bring to a boil. Reduce heat; cook and stir until thickened, about 2 minutes.

3. Add the gnocchi and chopped spinach; cook until spinach is wilted, 3-4 minutes. Add the chicken. Cover and simmer until heated through (do not boil), about 10 minutes.

NOTE: Look for potato gnocchi in the pasta or frozen foods section.

1 CUP: 482 cal., 28g fat (17g sat. fat), 125mg chol., 527mg sod., 36g carb. (10g sugars, 2g fiber), 21g pro.

SHRIMP PO'BOYS WITH PINEAPPLE SLAW

This great twist on the traditional po'boy sandwich adds healthy veggies while reducing fat and calories. For a smoked flavor, grill the shrimp. For a low-carb option, serve the po'boy open-faced on a baguette half.
—Melissa Pelkey Hass, Waleska, GA

TAKES: 30 min. • **MAKES:** 6 servings

- ⅓ cup egg substitute
- ½ cup panko (Japanese) bread crumbs
- 2 Tbsp. reduced-sodium Creole seasoning
- 1 lb. uncooked shrimp (16-20 per lb.), peeled and deveined
- 2 cups broccoli coleslaw mix
- 1 cup unsweetened pineapple tidbits, drained, 3 Tbsp. liquid reserved
- 2 green onions, chopped
- ½ cup reduced-fat mayonnaise
- 6 hoagie buns, split and toasted
- 4 Tbsp. reduced-fat tartar sauce
- 3 medium tomatoes, sliced

1. Preheat oven to 400°. Pour egg substitute into a shallow bowl. In a separate shallow bowl, mix bread crumbs and Creole seasoning. Dip shrimp in egg substitute, then in crumb mixture, patting to help coating adhere. Bake in a greased 15x10x1-in. pan until shrimp turn pink, 7-9 minutes. Keep warm.
2. Meanwhile, combine broccoli slaw, pineapple and green onions. In a small bowl, whisk together mayonnaise and reserved pineapple liquid until smooth. Add to the broccoli mixture; toss to coat.
3. To serve, spread hoagie buns with tartar sauce. Divide tomato slices and shrimp among buns. Top with pineapple broccoli slaw.
1 SANDWICH: 420 cal., 13g fat (2g sat. fat), 99mg chol., 1430mg sod., 54g carb. (15g sugars, 3g fiber), 23g pro.

ASIAN LETTUCE WRAPS

These wraps are as tasty as the those found in many popular restaurants. The bonus is these are healthier.
—Linda Rowley, Richardson, TX

INSPIRED BY:
P.F. CHANG'S
LETTUCE WRAPS

TAKES: 25 min. • **MAKES:** 4 servings

- 1   Tbsp. canola oil
- 1   lb. lean ground turkey
- 1   jalapeno pepper, seeded and minced
- 2   green onions, thinly sliced
- 2   garlic cloves, minced
- 2   Tbsp. minced fresh basil
- 2   Tbsp. lime juice
- 2   Tbsp. reduced-sodium soy sauce
- 1   to 2 Tbsp. chili garlic sauce
- 1   Tbsp. sugar or sugar substitute blend equivalent to 1 Tbsp. sugar
- 12 Bibb or Boston lettuce leaves
- 1   medium cucumber, julienned
- 1   medium carrot, julienned
- 2   cups bean sprouts

1. In a large skillet, heat oil over medium heat. Add turkey; cook 6-8 minutes or until no longer pink, breaking into crumbles. Add jalapeno, green onions and garlic; cook 2 minutes longer. Stir in basil, lime juice, soy sauce, chili garlic sauce and sugar; heat through.

2. To serve, place turkey mixture in lettuce leaves; top with cucumber, carrot and bean sprouts. Fold lettuce over filling.

3 LETTUCE WRAPS: 259 cal., 12g fat (3g sat. fat), 78mg chol., 503mg sod., 12g carb. (6g sugars, 3g fiber), 26g pro.
DIABETIC EXCHANGES: 3 lean meat, 1 vegetable, ½ starch, ½ fat.

FAVORITE BAKED POTATO SOUP

My husband and I enjoyed a delicious potato soup at a restaurant while on vacation and I came home determined to duplicate it. It took me five years to get the taste right!
—Joann Goetz, Genoa, OH

PREP: 20 min. • **BAKE:** 65 min. + cooling • **MAKES:** 10 servings

- 4 large baking potatoes (about 12 oz. each)
- ⅔ cup butter, cubed
- ⅔ cup all-purpose flour
- ¾ tsp. salt
- ¼ tsp. white pepper
- 6 cups 2% milk
- 1 cup sour cream
- ¼ cup thinly sliced green onions
- 1 cup shredded cheddar cheese
- 10 bacon strips, cooked and crumbled

1. Preheat oven to 350°. Pierce potatoes several times with a fork; place on a baking sheet. Bake until tender, 65-75 minutes. Cool completely.
2. Peel and cube potatoes. In a large saucepan, melt butter over medium heat. Stir in flour, salt and pepper until smooth; gradually whisk in milk. Bring to a boil, stirring constantly; cook and stir until thickened, about 2 minutes. Stir in potatoes; heat through.
3. Remove from heat; stir in sour cream and green onions. Top servings with cheese and bacon.
1 CUP: 469 cal., 28g fat (17g sat. fat), 86mg chol., 563mg sod., 41g carb. (10g sugars, 3g fiber), 14g pro.

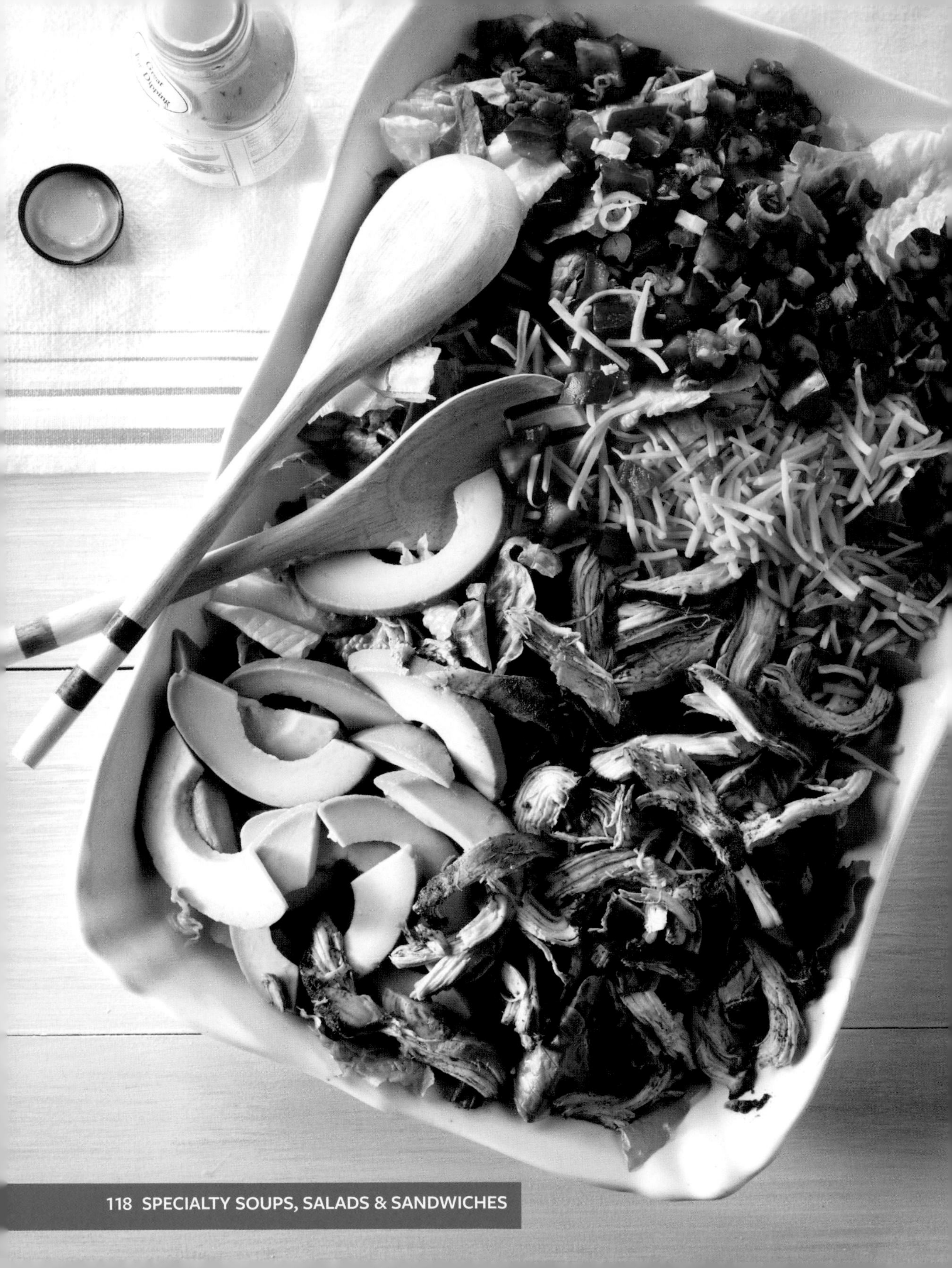
Great
for Dipping

SLOW-COOKER CHICKEN TACO SALAD

We use this slow-cooked chicken across several meals, including it in tacos, sandwiches, omelets and enchiladas. My little guys love helping measure the seasonings.
—Karie Houghton, Lynnwood, WA

PREP: 10 min. • **COOK:** 3 hours • **MAKES:** 6 servings

- 3 tsp. chili powder
- 1 tsp. each ground cumin, seasoned salt and pepper
- ½ tsp. each white pepper, ground chipotle pepper and paprika
- ¼ tsp. dried oregano
- ¼ tsp. crushed red pepper flakes
- 1½ lbs. boneless skinless chicken breasts
- 1 cup chicken broth
- 9 cups torn romaine
  Optional toppings: Sliced avocado, shredded cheddar cheese, chopped tomato, sliced green onions and ranch salad dressing

1. Mix seasonings; rub over chicken breasts. Place in a 3-qt. slow cooker. Add broth. Cook, covered, on low 3-4 hours or until chicken is tender.

2. Remove chicken; cool slightly. Shred with 2 forks. Serve over romaine; top as desired.

1¾ CUPS: 143 cal., 3g fat (1g sat. fat), 63mg chol., 516mg sod., 4g carb. (1g sugars, 2g fiber), 24g pro.
DIABETIC EXCHANGES: 3 lean meat, 1 vegetable.

INSPIRED BY:
CHIPOTLE'S CHICKEN SALAD

INSPIRED BY:
RED LOBSTER'S
NEW ENGLAND
CLAM CHOWDER

POTATO CLAM CHOWDER

I found this recipe in one of my vintage cookbooks. It's a timeless classic I prepare for friends and family throughout the year. We especially love it during the holidays.
—Betty Ann Morgan, Upper Marlboro, MD

PREP: 10 min. • **COOK:** 35 min. • **MAKES:** 6 servings

- 2 cans (6½ oz. each) minced clams
- 2 bacon strips, chopped
- 1 medium onion, chopped
- 2 Tbsp. all-purpose flour
- 1 cup water
- 1¾ lbs. potatoes (about 4 medium), peeled and cut into ¾-in. cubes
- ½ tsp. salt
- ¼ to ½ tsp. dried thyme
- ¼ tsp. dried savory
- ⅛ tsp. pepper
- 2 cups 2% milk
- 2 Tbsp. minced fresh parsley

1. Drain clams, reserving clam juice. In a large saucepan, cook bacon over medium heat until crisp, stirring occasionally. Remove bacon with a slotted spoon; drain on paper towels.
2. Add onion to drippings; cook and stir 4-6 minutes or until tender. Stir in flour until blended. Gradually stir in water and reserved clam juice; cook and stir until bubbly.
3. Add potatoes and seasonings; bring to a boil, stirring frequently. Reduce heat; simmer, covered, 20-25 minutes or until potatoes are tender, stirring occasionally.
4. Stir in milk, parsley and clams; heat through. Top with bacon.
1 CUP: 201 cal., 6g fat (2g sat. fat), 34mg chol., 615mg sod., 27g carb. (6g sugars, 2g fiber), 11g pro.
DIABETIC EXCHANGES: 2 starch, 2 lean meat.

CHICKEN CROISSANT SANDWICHES

These are easy to pull together when you need something fun and company-worthy in a flash. I make them often for family brunches, church youth meetings and impromptu gatherings with friends.
—Cheryl Sigler, Louisville, OH

TAKES: 15 min. • **MAKES:** 4 servings

⅓ cup mayonnaise
¼ tsp. ground ginger
¼ tsp. ground mustard
   Dash salt
1½ cups diced cooked chicken
⅓ cup diced apple
⅓ cup sunflower kernels
2 green onions, finely chopped
⅓ cup mandarin oranges
4 croissants, split
   Lettuce leaves, optional

In a small bowl, mix mayonnaise, ginger, mustard and salt. Stir in chicken, apple, sunflower kernels and green onions. Gently fold in mandarin oranges. Serve on croissants with lettuce if desired.
1 SANDWICH: 537 cal., 35g fat (11g sat. fat), 86mg chol., 527mg sod., 34g carb. (11g sugars, 3g fiber), 23g pro.

WEDGE SALAD WITH BLUE CHEESE DRESSING

A classic wedge salad gets an indulgent treatment when topped with a homemade blue cheese dressing and crumbled bacon.
—Jenn Smith, Rumford, RI

TAKES: 20 min. • **MAKES:** 6 servings

- ⅔ **cup crumbled blue cheese**
- ⅔ **cup mayonnaise**
- ⅓ **cup reduced-fat sour cream**
- 2 **tsp. water**
- 1½ **tsp. red wine vinegar**
- ⅛ **tsp. Worcestershire sauce**
   Dash cayenne pepper
- 1 **large head iceberg lettuce**
- 2 **cups chopped assorted tomatoes**
- 6 **bacon strips, cooked and crumbled**

In a small bowl, mix the first 7 ingredients. Cut lettuce into 6 wedges. To serve, top wedges with dressing, tomatoes and bacon.
1 SERVING: 313 cal., 28g fat (7g sat. fat), 33mg chol., 473mg sod., 6g carb. (4g sugars, 2g fiber), 8g pro.

CRUNCHY ASIAN CHICKEN SALAD

I love this crunchy, citrusy salad. One day I had my husband drive an hour to the nearest Applebee's restaurant just so I could eat it! That's when I decided to come up with my own version that's a great stand-in for the original. I'm happy and my husband is, too!
—Mandy Bird, Holbrook, ID

INSPIRED BY:
APPLEBEE'S
ORIENTAL CHICKEN SALAD

TAKES: 25 min. • **MAKES:** 4 servings

- 4 frozen breaded chicken tenders (about 8 oz.)
- ⅓ cup mayonnaise
- 3 Tbsp. honey
- 2 Tbsp. rice vinegar
- 1½ tsp. Dijon mustard
- ¼ tsp. sesame oil
- 1 pkg. (10 oz.) hearts of romaine salad mix
- 1 pkg. (14 oz.) coleslaw mix
- ¼ cup crispy chow mein noodles
- ⅓ cup sliced almonds, toasted

1. Cook chicken tenders according to the package directions. Meanwhile, whisk together mayonnaise, honey, vinegar, mustard and sesame oil.

2. To serve, place romaine and coleslaw mixes in a large bowl; toss with dressing. Divide among 4 plates. Cut the chicken into bite-sized pieces; place over salads. Sprinkle with chow mein noodles and almonds.

NOTE: To toast nuts, bake in a shallow pan in a 350° oven for 5 10 minutes or cook in a skillet over low heat until lightly browned, stirring occasionally.

1 SERVING: 419 cal., 25g fat (3g sat. fat), 11mg chol., 602mg sod., 42g carb. (20g sugars, 7g fiber), 12g pro.

SLOW-COOKED CHILI

This hearty chili can cook for up to 10 hours on low in the slow cooker. It's so good to come home to its wonderful aroma after a long day away.
—Sue Call, Beech Grove, IN

PREP: 20 min. • **COOK:** 8 hours • **MAKES:** 10 servings (2½ qt.)

- 2 lbs. lean ground beef (90% lean)
- 2 cans (16 oz. each) kidney beans, rinsed and drained
- 2 cans (14½ oz. each) diced tomatoes, undrained
- 1 can (8 oz.) tomato sauce
- 2 medium onions, chopped
- 1 green pepper, chopped
- 2 garlic cloves, minced
- 2 Tbsp. chili powder
- 1 tsp. salt
- 1 tsp. pepper
  Shredded cheddar cheese and thinly sliced green onions, optional

1. In a large skillet, cook ground beef over medium heat until no longer pink; drain.
2. Transfer to a 5-qt. slow cooker. Add the next 9 ingredients. Cover and cook on low for 8-10 hours. If desired, top individual servings with cheese and green onions.
1 CUP: 260 cal., 8g fat (3g sat. fat), 57mg chol., 712mg sod., 23g carb. (6g sugars, 7g fiber), 25g pro.
DIABETIC EXCHANGES: 3 lean meat, 1½ starch, 1 vegetable.

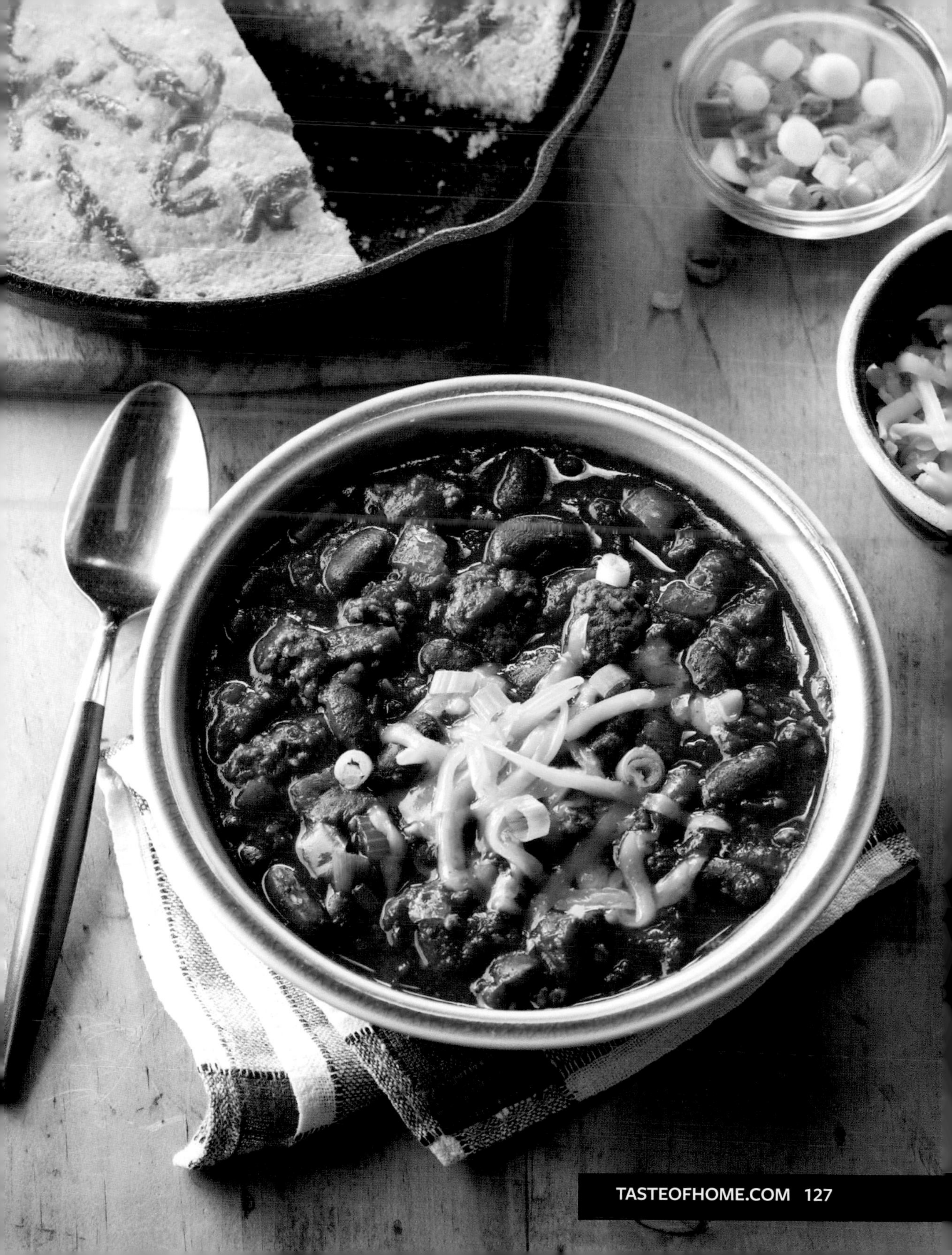

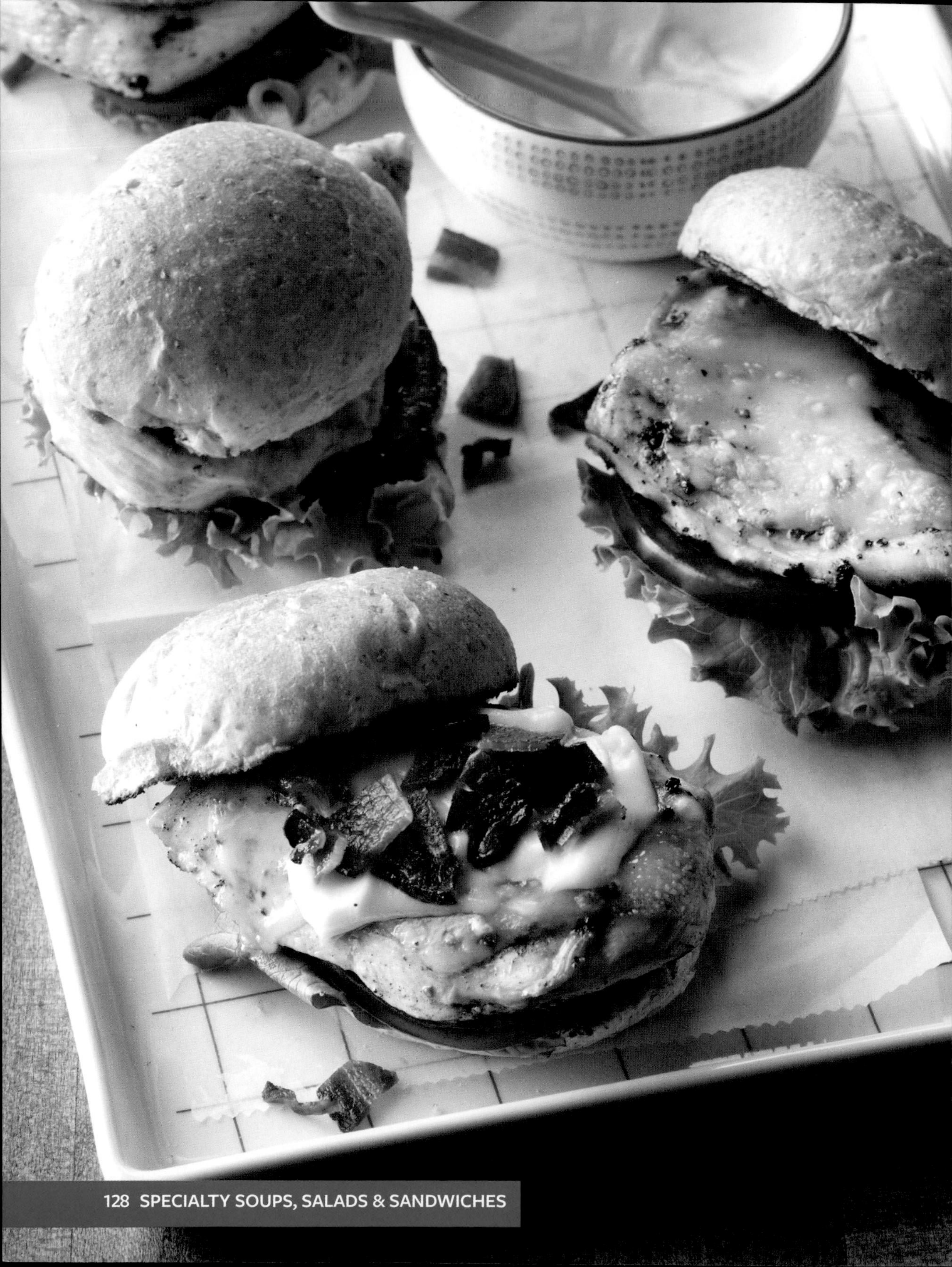

BACON & SWISS CHICKEN SANDWICHES

I created this sandwich based on one my daughter ordered at a restaurant. She likes to dip her sandwich in the extra honey-mustard sauce.
—Marilyn Moberg, Papillion, NE

TAKES: 25 min. • **MAKES:** 4 servings

- ¼ cup reduced-fat mayonnaise
- 1 Tbsp. Dijon mustard
- 1 Tbsp. honey
- 4 boneless skinless chicken breast halves (4 oz. each)
- ½ tsp. Montreal steak seasoning
- 4 slices Swiss cheese
- 4 whole wheat hamburger buns, split
- 2 bacon strips, cooked and crumbled
  Lettuce leaves and tomato slices, optional

1. In a small bowl, mix mayonnaise, mustard and honey. Pound chicken with a meat mallet to ½-in. thickness. Sprinkle chicken with steak seasoning. Grill chicken, covered, over medium heat or broil 4 in. from heat until a thermometer reads 165°, 4-6 minutes on each side Top with cheese during the last 1 minute of cooking.
2. Grill buns over medium heat, cut side down, until toasted, 30-60 seconds. Serve chicken on buns with bacon, mayonnaise mixture and, if desired, lettuce and tomato.

1 SANDWICH: 410 cal., 17g fat (6g sat. fat), 91mg chol., 667mg sod., 29g carb. (9g sugars, 3g fiber), 34g pro.
DIABETIC EXCHANGES: 4 lean meat, 2 starch, 2 fat.

HEARTY PASTA FAGIOLI

Here's an Italian favorite. Convenient jarred spaghetti sauce and canned broth form the flavorful base. Add breadsticks and a crisp green salad and you have a meal!
—Cindy Garland, Limestone, TN

Prep: 40 min. • **Cook:** 40 min. • **Makes:** 24 servings (7½ qt.)

- 2 lbs. ground beef
- 6 cans (14½ oz. each) beef broth
- 2 cans (28 oz. each) diced tomatoes, undrained
- 2 jars (26 oz. each) spaghetti sauce
- 3 large onions, chopped
- 8 celery ribs, diced
- 3 medium carrots, sliced
- 1 can (16 oz.) kidney beans, rinsed and drained
- 1 can (15 oz.) cannellini beans, rinsed and drained
- 3 tsp. minced fresh oregano or 1 tsp. dried oregano
- 2½ tsp. pepper
- 1½ tsp. hot pepper sauce
- 8 oz. uncooked medium pasta shells
- 5 tsp. minced fresh parsley

1. In a large stockpot, cook beef over medium heat until no longer pink; drain. Add broth, tomatoes, spaghetti sauce, onions, celery, carrots, beans, oregano, pepper and pepper sauce.
2. Bring to a boil. Reduce heat; simmer, covered, for 30 minutes. Add pasta and minced parsley; simmer, covered, until pasta is tender, 10-14 minutes.
1¼ CUPS: 212 cal., 6g fat (2g sat. fat), 20mg chol., 958mg sod., 25g carb. (8g sugars, 5g fiber), 14g pro.

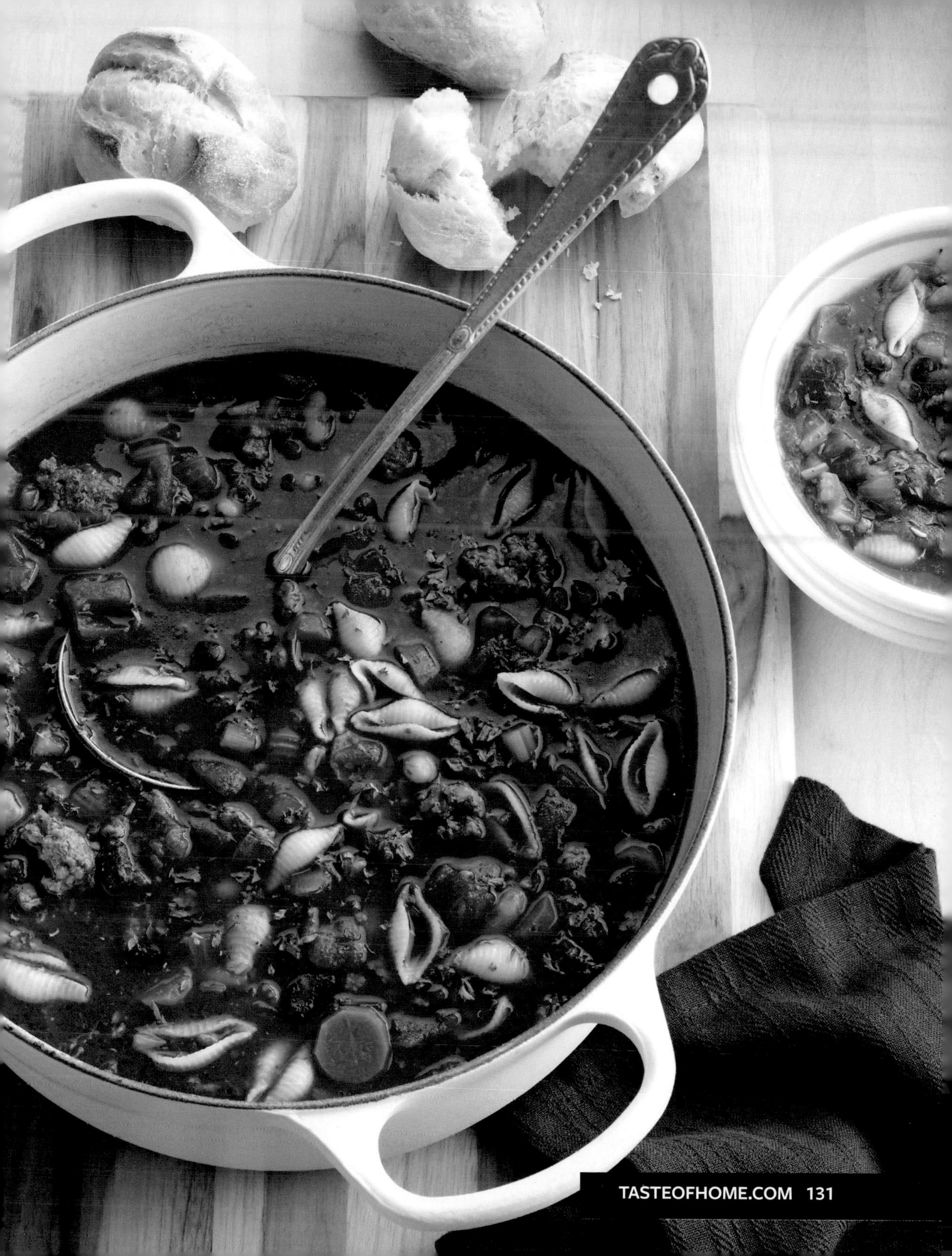

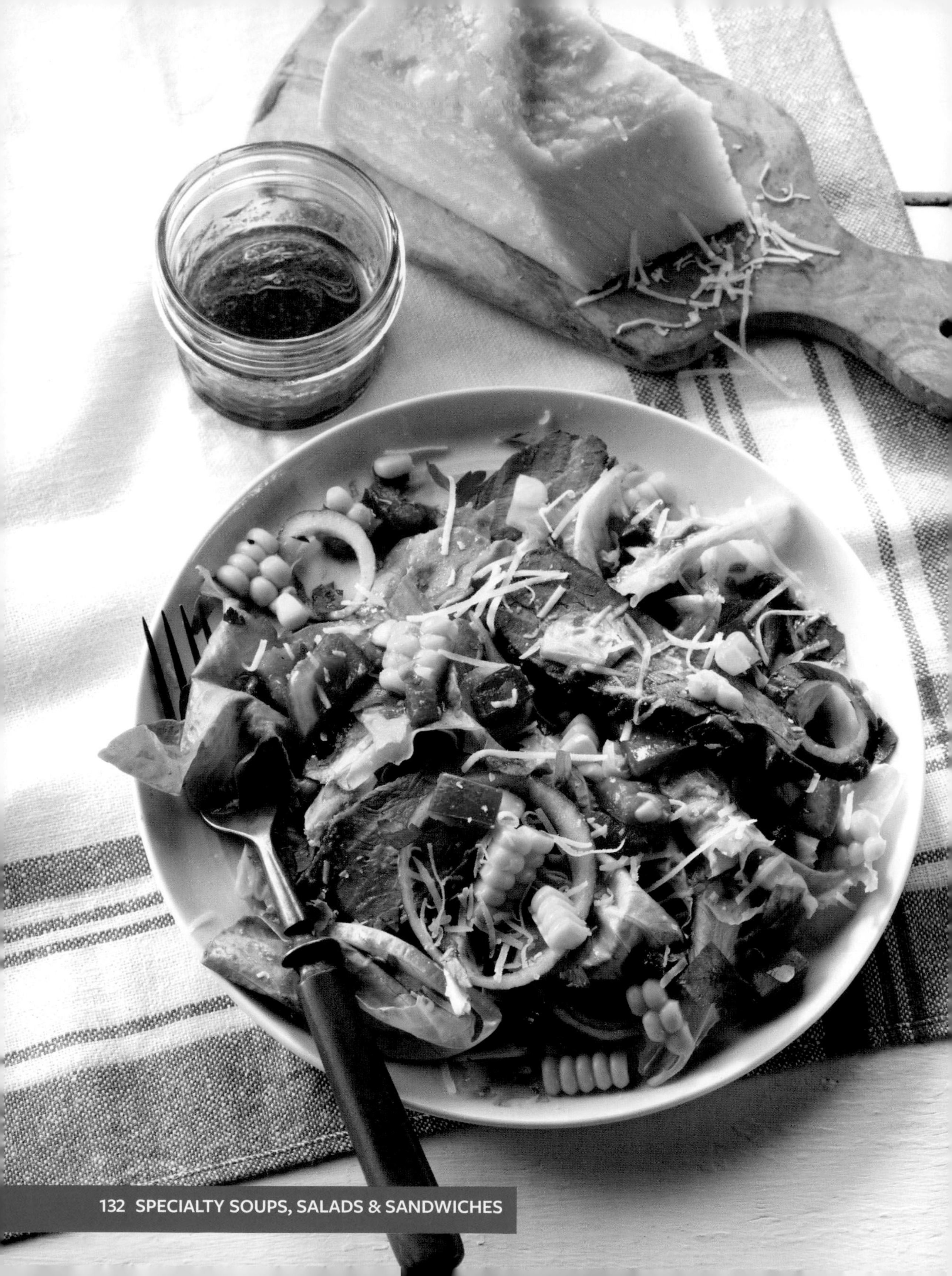

VEGGIE STEAK SALAD

This salad explodes with flavor. It's quick and easy to prepare and a healthy option, too.
—Tiffany Martinez, Aliso Viejo, CA

TAKES: 30 min. • **MAKES:** 5 servings

- 2 medium ears sweet corn, husked
- 1 beef flank steak (1 lb.)
- ¼ tsp. salt
- ¼ tsp. pepper
- 2 Tbsp. olive oil

DRESSING

- 2 Tbsp. olive oil
- 2 Tbsp. balsamic vinegar
- 1 tsp. garlic powder
- 1 tsp. capers, drained
- 1 tsp. Dijon mustard

SALAD

- 1 pkg. (5 oz.) spring mix salad greens
- 1 large tomato, chopped
- 4 slices red onion, separated into rings
- ¼ cup minced fresh parsley
- ¼ cup shredded Parmesan cheese

1. In a pot of boiling water, cook corn, uncovered, until tender, 3-5 minutes. Remove; cool slightly. Cut corn from cobs.

2. Sprinkle flank steak with salt and pepper. In a large skillet, heat 2 Tbsp. olive oil over medium heat. Add steak; cook until a thermometer reads 135° for medium-rare, 6-8 minutes per side. Remove from heat; let stand 5 minutes.

3. In a small bowl, whisk together dressing ingredients. Thinly slice steak across the grain. Place greens, tomato, onion, parsley, corn and steak in a large bowl; toss with dressing. Sprinkle with cheese.

2 CUPS: 301 cal., 19g fat (5g sat. fat), 46mg chol., 301mg sod., 12g carb. (5g sugars, 2g fiber), 21g pro.
DIABETIC EXCHANGES: 3 lean meat, 2½ fat, 2 vegetable.

INSPIRED BY:
TEXAS ROADHOUSE'S
HOUSE SALAD

BACON-TOMATO SALAD

We love this wonderful salad that tastes like a piled-high BLT without the time, effort or carbs. You can make it hours ahead and keep it in the fridge until serving time.
—Denise Thurman, Columbia, MO

TAKES: 15 min. • **MAKES:** 6 servings

1 pkg. (12 oz.) iceberg lettuce blend
2 cups grape tomatoes, halved
¾ cup coleslaw salad dressing
¾ cup shredded cheddar cheese
12 bacon strips, cooked and crumbled

In a large bowl, combine lettuce blend and tomatoes. Drizzle with dressing; sprinkle with cheese and bacon.
1¼ CUPS: 268 cal., 20g fat (6g sat. fat), 41mg chol., 621mg sod., 11g carb. (9g sugars, 1g fiber), 10g pro.

CREAMY COLESLAW

A convenient package of coleslaw mix cuts down on the prep time for this recipe. That makes it a winner in my book! It's great for potlucks or a busy weeknight when you have to get supper on the table fast.
—Renee Endress, Galva, IL

TAKES: 10 min. • **MAKES:** 6 servings

- 1 pkg. (14 oz.) coleslaw mix
- ¾ cup mayonnaise
- ⅓ cup sour cream
- ¼ cup sugar
- ¾ tsp. seasoned salt
- ½ tsp. ground mustard
- ¼ tsp. celery salt

Place coleslaw mix in a large bowl. In a small bowl, combine the remaining ingredients; stir until blended. Pour over coleslaw mix and toss to coat. Refrigerate until serving.

¾ CUP: 283 cal., 24g fat (5g sat. fat), 19mg chol., 431mg sod., 13g carb. (11g sugars, 2g fiber), 1g pro.

INSPIRED BY:
CULVER'S
COLESLAW

HAVE IT YOUR WAY

For a change of pace, try this recipe with broccoli slaw mix. Greek yogurt can be used instead of sour cream for less fat and more protein. If you like your coleslaw tart, add ¼ cup vinegar or lemon juice or a julienned Granny Smith apple.

BISTRO TURKEY SANDWICH

As a turkey lover who can't get enough during fall and winter, I was inspired to come up with a restaurant-worthy sandwich. I love it with a soft, rich cheese like Brie.
—Grace Voltolina, Westport, CT

TAKES: 30 min. • **MAKES:** 4 servings

- 2 Tbsp. butter, divided
- 1 large Granny Smith or Honeycrisp apple, cut into ¼-in. slices
- ½ tsp. sugar
- ¼ tsp. ground cinnamon
- ½ medium sweet onion, sliced
- ¼ cup whole-berry or jellied cranberry sauce
- 4 ciabatta rolls, split
- 1 lb. cooked turkey, sliced
- 8 slices Camembert or Brie cheese (about 8 oz.)
- 3 cups arugula (about 2 oz.)

1. Preheat broiler. In a large skillet, heat 1 Tbsp. butter over medium heat; saute apple slices with sugar and cinnamon until crisp-tender, 3-4 minutes. Remove from pan.

2. In same pan, melt remaining butter over medium heat; saute onion until lightly browned, 3-4 minutes. Remove from heat; stir in sauteed apple.

3. Spread cranberry sauce onto cut side of bottom portion of rolls; layer with turkey, apple mixture and cheese. Place on a baking sheet alongside roll tops, cut side up.

4. Broil 3-4 in. from heat until cheese begins to melt and roll tops are golden brown, 45-60 seconds. Add arugula; close sandwiches.

1 SANDWICH: 797 cal., 28g fat (14g sat. fat), 171mg chol., 1196mg sod., 87g carb. (16g sugars, 6g fiber), 55g pro.

Copycat Entrees

DIG IN! WITH THESE COPYCAT RECIPES, IT'S A SNAP TO SERVE THE SIGNATURE ENTREES FROM YOUR FAVORITE EATERIES. TURN HERE FOR CASUAL MEALS, WEEKEND SPECIALTIES AND EVERYTHING IN BETWEEN!

WISCONSIN BUTTER-BASTED
BURGERS, P. 175
INSPIRED BY: CULVER'S
BUTTERBURGER "THE ORIGINAL"

ZIPPY CHICKEN ENCHILADAS

Leftover chicken gets a flavorful upgrade in this rich and creamy casserole. It's a nice change of pace from beef enchiladas.
—Julie Moutray, Wichita, KS

PREP: 15 min. • **BAKE:** 35 min. • **MAKES:** 10 servings

- 1 can (16 oz.) refried beans
- 10 flour tortillas (8 in.), warmed
- 1 can (10¾ oz.) condensed cream of chicken soup, undiluted
- 1 cup sour cream
- 3 to 4 cups cubed cooked chicken
- 3 cups shredded cheddar cheese, divided
- 1 can (15 oz.) enchilada sauce
- ¼ cup sliced green onions
- ¼ cup sliced ripe olives
  Shredded lettuce, optional

1. Spread about 2 Tbsp. of beans on each tortilla. Combine soup and sour cream; stir in the chicken. Spoon ⅓ to ½ cup down the center of each tortilla; top with 1 Tbsp. cheese.
2. Roll up and place seam side down in a greased 13x9-in. baking dish. Pour enchilada sauce over top; sprinkle with the onions, olives and remaining cheese.
3. Bake, uncovered, at 350° for about 35 minutes or until heated through. Just before serving, sprinkle lettuce around enchiladas if desired.

FREEZE OPTION: Cover and freeze unbaked casserole. To use, partially thaw in refrigerator overnight. Remove from refrigerator 30 minutes before baking. Preheat oven to 350°. Bake casserole as directed, increasing time as necessary to heat through and for a thermometer inserted in center to read 165°.

1 SERVING: 487 cal., 23g fat (12g sat. fat), 95mg chol., 1001mg sod., 39g carb. (3g sugars, 4g fiber), 29g pro.

INSPIRED BY:
THE CHEESECAKE FACTORY'S
CHICKEN ENCHILADAS

CAJUN BAKED CATFISH

This well-seasoned fish gets me compliments from family and friends whenever I serve it. It's moist and flaky with a crispy coating.
—Jim Gales, Milwaukee, WI

TAKES: 25 min. • **MAKES:** 2 servings

- 2   Tbsp. yellow cornmeal
- 2   tsp. Cajun or blackened seasoning
- ½   tsp. dried thyme
- ½   tsp. dried basil
- ¼   tsp. garlic powder
- ¼   tsp. lemon-pepper seasoning
- 2   catfish or tilapia fillets (6 oz. each)
- ¼   tsp. paprika

1. Preheat oven to 400°. In a shallow bowl, mix the first 6 ingredients.
2. Dip fillets in cornmeal mixture to coat both sides. Place on a baking sheet coated with cooking spray. Sprinkle with paprika.
3. Bake until fish begins to flake easily with fork, 20-25 minutes.

1 FILLET: 242 cal., 10g fat (2g sat. fat), 94mg chol., 748mg sod., 8g carb. (0 sugars, 1g fiber), 27g pro.
DIABETIC EXCHANGES: 4 lean meat, ½ starch.

BANDITO CHILI DOGS

These deluxe chili dogs are a surefire hit at family functions. Adults and children alike love the cheesy chili sauce and fun toppings!
—Marlon Lowery, Medford, OR

PREP: 15 min. • **COOK:** 4 hours • **MAKES:** 10 servings

- 1 pkg. (1 lb.) hot dogs
- 2 cans (15 oz. each) chili without beans
- 1 can (10¾ oz.) condensed cheddar cheese soup, undiluted
- 1 can (4 oz.) chopped green chiles
- 10 hot dog buns, split
- 1 medium onion, chopped
- 1 to 2 cups corn chips, coarsely crushed
- 1 cup shredded cheddar cheese

1. Place hot dogs in a 3-qt. slow cooker. In a large bowl, combine the chili, soup and green chiles; pour over hot dogs. Cover and cook on low for 4-5 hours.

2. Serve hot dogs in buns; top with chili mixture, onion, corn chips and cheese.

1 CHILI DOG: 450 cal., 23g fat (10g sat. fat), 53mg chol., 1442mg sod., 43g carb. (6g sugars, 3g fiber), 19g pro.

QUICK CHICKEN & DUMPLINGS

Oh, the things you can make with frozen biscuit dough! I use buttermilk biscuits to make this easy dumpling dish.
—Lakeya Astwood, Schenectady, NY

TAKES: 30 min. • **MAKES:** 6 servings

- 6 **individually frozen biscuits**
- ¼ **cup chopped onion**
- ¼ **cup chopped green pepper**
- 1 **Tbsp. olive oil**
- 4 **cups shredded rotisserie chicken**
- 3 **cans (14½ oz. each) reduced-sodium chicken broth**
- 1 **can (4 oz.) mushroom stems and pieces, drained**
- 1 **tsp. chicken bouillon granules**
- 1 **tsp. minced fresh parsley**
- ½ **tsp. dried sage leaves**
- ¼ **tsp. dried rosemary, crushed**
- ¼ **tsp. pepper**

1. Cut each biscuit into fourths; set aside. In a large saucepan, saute onion and green pepper in oil until tender. Stir in the chicken, broth, mushrooms, bouillon granules, parsley, sage, rosemary and pepper.
2. Bring to a boil. Reduce heat; add the biscuit pieces for dumplings. Cover and simmer until a toothpick inserted in the center of a dumpling comes out clean (do not lift cover while simmering), about 10 minutes.

1½ CUPS: 420 cal., 20g fat (5g sat. fat), 83mg chol., 1443mg sod., 26g carb. (6g sugars, 1g fiber), 34g pro.

SPICE-RUBBED SALMON

We enjoy this salmon with couscous and fresh veggies. It's become a regular on the dinner rotation. Even my 2-year-old devours it!
—Lyndsay Rensing, Katy, TX

TAKES: 20 min. • **MAKES:** 4 servings

- 1 tsp. brown sugar
- 1 tsp. ground cumin
- ½ tsp. salt
- ½ tsp. dried parsley flakes
- ½ tsp. chili powder
- ¼ tsp. garlic powder
- ¼ tsp. ground mustard
- ¼ tsp. paprika
- ¼ tsp. pepper
- ⅛ tsp. ground cinnamon
- 4 salmon fillets (6 oz. each)
- 2 tsp. olive oil

1. In a small bowl, mix the first 10 ingredients. Rub fillets with seasoning mixture; drizzle with oil.
2. Place salmon on lightly oiled rack, skin side up. Grill, covered, over high heat or broil 3-4 in. from heat 5 minutes. Turn; grill 4-6 minutes longer or until fish just begins to flake easily with a fork.

1 FILLET: 295 cal., 18g fat (3g sat. fat), 85mg chol., 385mg sod., 2g carb. (1g sugars, 0 fiber), 29g pro.
DIABETIC EXCHANGES: 5 lean meat, ½ fat.

CRISPY ORANGE CHICKEN

These tangy Asian-inspired nuggets can be served a variety of ways. We eat them over noodles or rice, in sandwiches, even on top of lettuce and cabbage.
—Darlene Brenden, Salem, OR

TAKES: 30 min. • **MAKES:** 4 servings

- 16 oz. frozen popcorn chicken (about 4 cups)
- 1 Tbsp. canola oil
- 2 medium carrots, thinly sliced
- 1 garlic clove, minced
- 1½ tsp. grated orange zest
- 1 cup orange juice
- ⅓ cup hoisin sauce
- 3 Tbsp. sugar
- ¼ tsp. salt
- ¼ tsp. pepper
  Dash cayenne pepper
  Hot cooked rice

1. Bake popcorn chicken according to package directions.
2. Meanwhile, in a large skillet, heat oil over medium-high heat. Add carrots; cook and stir 3-5 minutes or until tender. Add garlic; cook 1 minute longer. Stir in the orange zest, juice, hoisin sauce, sugar and seasonings; bring to a boil. Reduce heat; simmer, uncovered, 4-6 minutes or until thickened, stirring constantly.
3. Add chicken to skillet; toss to coat. Serve with rice.

1 CUP: 450 cal., 20g fat (3g sat. fat), 35mg chol., 1294mg sod., 56g carb. (25g sugars, 3g fiber), 14g pro.

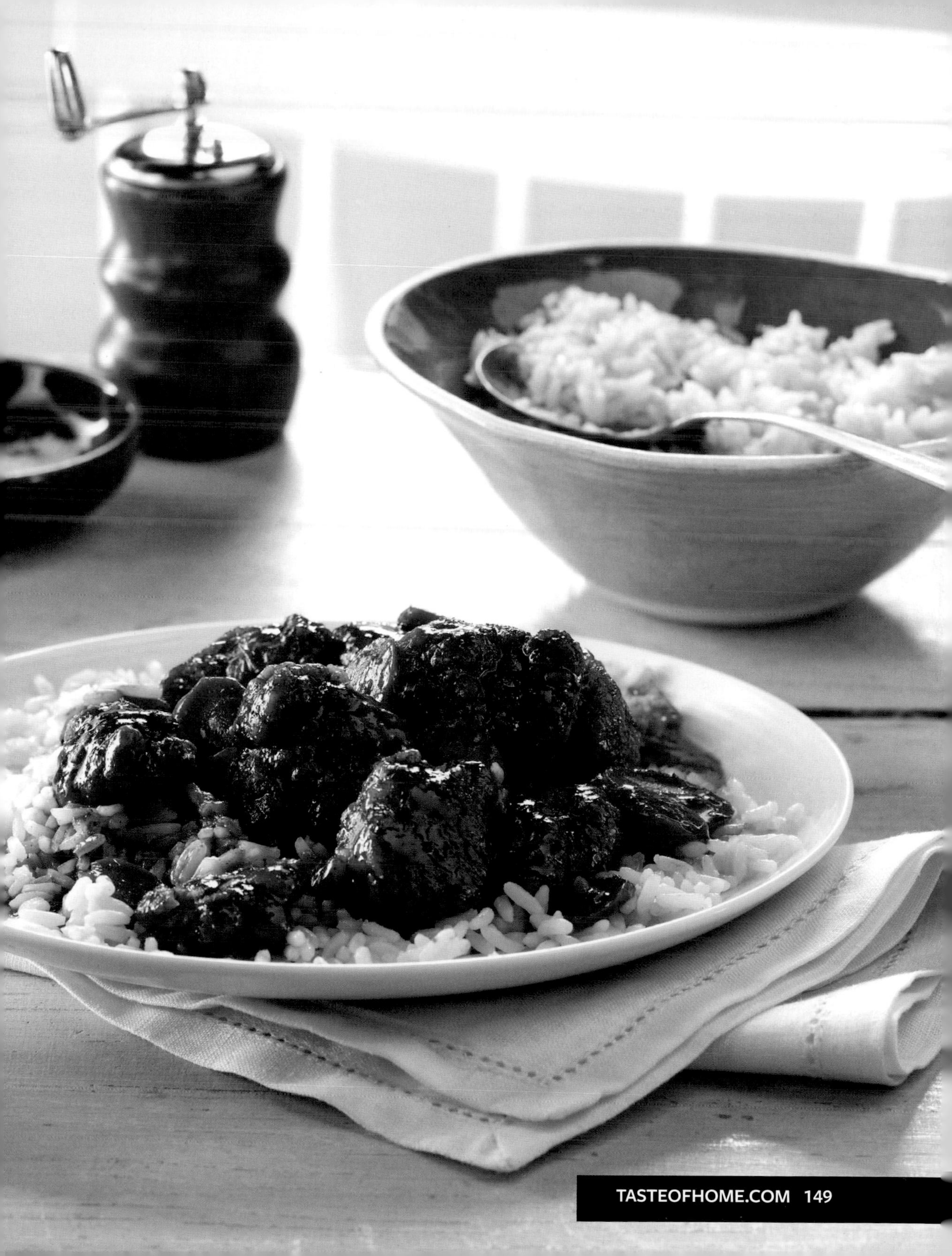

BIG JOHN'S CHILI-RUBBED RIBS

When my family thinks of summer grilling, it's ribs all the way. Our Asian-inspired recipe is a welcome change from the usual barbecue-sauce versions.
—Ginger Sullivan, Cutler Bay, FL

PREP: 20 min. + chilling • **GRILL:** 1½ hours • **MAKES:** 10 servings

- 3 Tbsp. packed brown sugar
- 2 Tbsp. paprika
- 2 Tbsp. chili powder
- 3 tsp. ground cumin
- 2 tsp. garlic powder
- 1 tsp. salt
- 6 lbs. pork baby back ribs

GLAZE
- 1 cup reduced-sodium soy sauce
- 1 cup packed brown sugar
- ⅔ cup ketchup
- ⅓ cup lemon juice
- 1½ tsp. minced fresh gingerroot

1. Mix the first 6 ingredients; rub over ribs. Refrigerate, covered, 30 minutes.
2. Wrap rib racks in large pieces of heavy-duty foil; seal tightly. Grill, covered, over indirect medium heat until meat is tender, 1-1½ hours.
3. In a large saucepan, combine the glaze ingredients; cook, uncovered, over medium heat until heated through and sugar is dissolved, 6-8 minutes, stirring occasionally.
4. Carefully remove ribs from foil. Place ribs over direct heat; brush with some of the glaze. Grill, covered, over medium heat until browned, 25-30 minutes, turning and brushing the ribs occasionally with remaining glaze.

1 SERVING: 486 cal., 26g fat (9g sat. fat), 98mg chol., 1543mg sod., 34g carb. (30g sugars, 1g fiber), 29g pro.

INDIANA-STYLE CORN DOGS

One of the best things about the many fairs and festivals in Indiana is the corn dogs! We adore them, so they're a regular in our house.
—Sally Denney, Warsaw, IN

PREP: 20 min. • **COOK:** 5 min./batch • **MAKES:** 12 corn dogs

- 1 cup all-purpose flour
- ½ cup yellow cornmeal
- 1 Tbsp. sugar
- 3 tsp. baking powder
- 1 tsp. salt
- ½ tsp. ground mustard
- ¼ tsp. paprika
  Dash pepper
- 1 large egg, lightly beaten
- 1 cup evaporated milk
  Oil for deep-fat frying
- 12 wooden skewers
- 12 hot dogs

1. In a bowl, whisk the first 8 ingredients. Whisk in egg and milk just until blended. Transfer batter to a tall drinking glass.
2. In an electric skillet or deep-fat fryer, heat oil to 375°. Insert the skewers into hot dogs. Dip hot dogs into batter; allow excess batter to drip off. Fry corn dogs, a few at a time, 2-3 minutes or until golden brown, turning occasionally. Drain corn dogs on paper towels. Serve immediately.

1 CORN DOG: 299 cal., 21g fat (7g sat. fat), 47mg chol., 805mg sod., 18g carb. (4g sugars, 1g fiber), 9g pro.

INSPIRED BY:
HARD ROCK CAFE'S
GRILLED NORWEGIAN SALMON

EASY GLAZED SALMON

It only takes four ingredients and fewer than 30 minutes to make this delightful main dish.
—Tara Ernspiker, Falling Waters, WV

TAKES: 25 min. • **MAKES:** 4 servings

- ⅓ cup packed brown sugar
- ¼ cup unsweetened pineapple juice
- 2 Tbsp. soy sauce
- 4 salmon fillets (6 oz. each)

1. Line a 15x10x1-in. baking pan with foil; grease the foil. Set aside. In a small bowl, combine the brown sugar, pineapple juice and soy sauce. Place salmon skin side down on prepared pan. Spoon sauce mixture over fish.

2. Bake, uncovered, at 350° for 20-25 minutes or until fish flakes easily with a fork, basting frequently with pan juices.

1 FILLET: 394 cal., 18g fat (4g sat. fat), 100mg chol., 568mg sod., 20g carb. (19g sugars, 0 fiber), 35g pro.

CHEDDAR CHILI BURGERS

Savory chili and french-fried onions are a fun alternative to the traditional burger fixings of ketchup and mustard. The patties are easy to assemble, making them a great weeknight dinner.
—Sue Ross, Casa Grande, AZ

TAKES: 20 min. • **MAKES:** 4 servings

- 1 lb. ground beef
- 1½ tsp. chili powder
- 1 can (15 oz.) chili with beans
- 4 hamburger buns, split and toasted
- ½ cup shredded cheddar cheese
- 1 can (2.8 oz.) french-fried onions

1. In a large bowl, combine beef and chili powder. Shape into 4 patties. Pan-fry, grill or broil until meat is no longer pink.
2. Meanwhile, in a small saucepan, bring chili to a boil. Reduce heat; simmer for 5 minutes or until heated through. Place burgers on bun bottoms; top with chili, cheese and onions. Replace bun tops.

1 SERVING: 584 cal., 28g fat (12g sat. fat), 81mg chol., 1081mg sod., 46g carb. (5g sugars, 5g fiber), 34g pro.

INSPIRED BY:
RED ROBIN'S
CHILI CHILI CHEESEBURGER

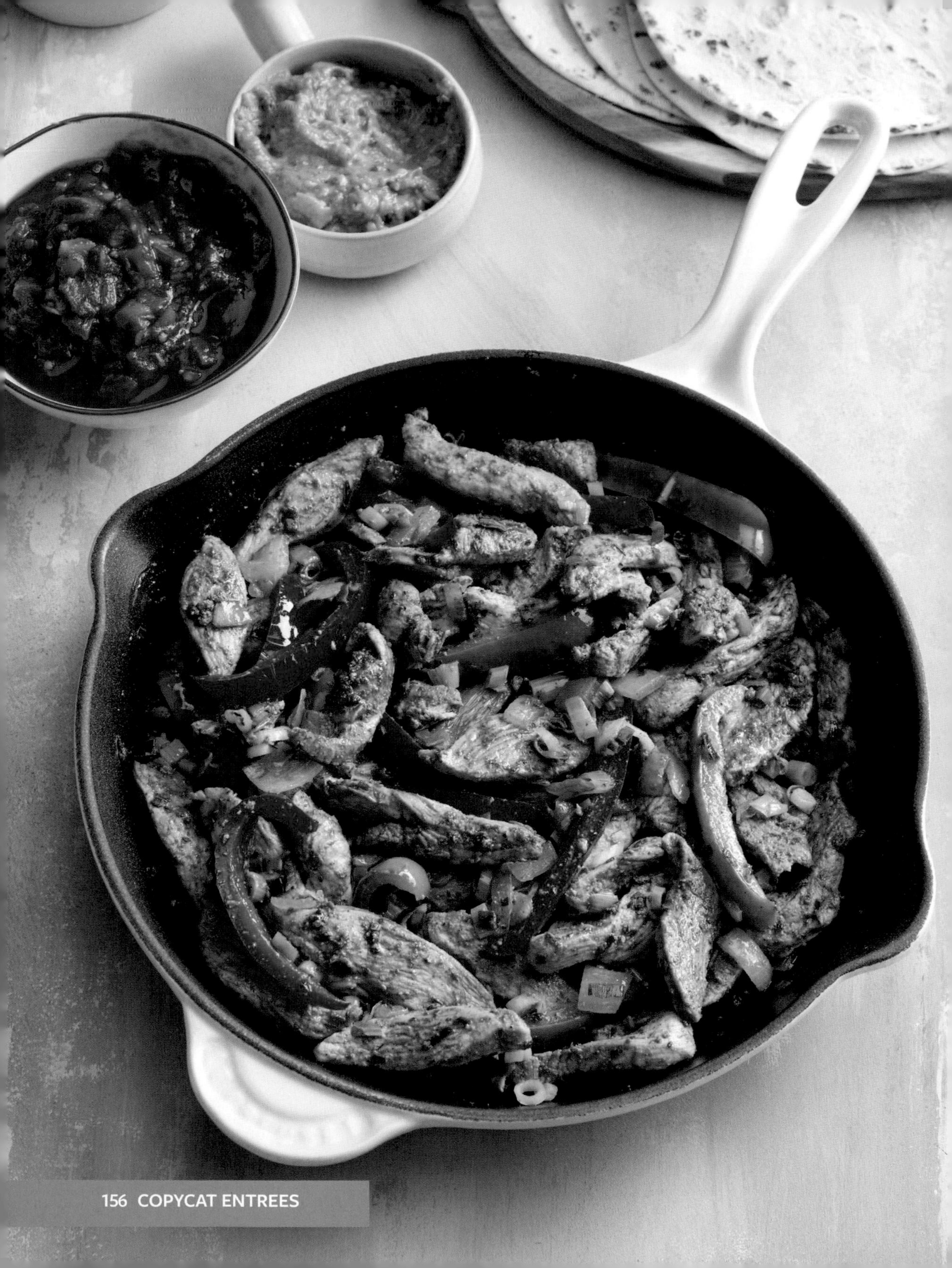

FLAVORFUL CHICKEN FAJITAS

The marinated chicken in these popular wraps is mouthwatering.
They go together in a snap and always get raves!
—Julie Sterchi, Campbellsville, KY

PREP: 20 min. + marinating • **COOK:** 10 min. • **MAKES:** 6 servings

- 4 Tbsp. canola oil, divided
- 2 Tbsp. lemon juice
- 1½ tsp. seasoned salt
- 1½ tsp. dried oregano
- 1½ tsp. ground cumin
- 1 tsp. garlic powder
- ½ tsp. chili powder
- ½ tsp. paprika
- ½ tsp. crushed red pepper flakes, optional
- 1½ lbs. boneless skinless chicken breast, cut into thin strips
- ½ medium sweet red pepper, julienned
- ¼ medium green pepper, julienned
- 4 green onions, thinly sliced
- ½ cup chopped onion
- 6 flour tortillas (8 in.), warmed
  Optional: Shredded cheddar cheese, taco sauce, salsa, guacamole and sour cream

1. In a large bowl, combine 2 Tbsp. oil, lemon juice and seasonings; add chicken. Turn to coat; cover. Refrigerate for 1-4 hours.
2. In a large skillet, saute peppers and onions in remaining oil until crisp-tender. Remove and keep warm.
3. Drain chicken, discarding marinade. In the same skillet, cook chicken over medium-high heat for 5-6 minutes or until no longer pink. Return pepper mixture to pan; heat through.
4. Spoon filling down the center of tortillas; fold in half. Serve with toppings as desired.

1 FAJITA: 369 cal., 15g fat (2g sat. fat), 63mg chol., 689mg sod., 30g carb. (2g sugars, 1g fiber), 28g pro.
DIABETIC EXCHANGES: 3 lean meat, 2 starch, 2 fat.

HAVE IT YOUR WAY
Oregano is used frequently in Latin American cuisine. Mexican oregano has a more citrusy, peppery bite but is similar in flavor to the sweeter Mediterranean oregano. Either variety will work in this recipe.

MOM'S ROAST BEEF

Everyone loves slices of this fork-tender roast beef and its savory gravy. This well-seasoned roast is Mom's specialty. People always ask what her secret ingredients are. Now you have the delicious recipe for our favorite meat dish!
—Linda Gaido, New Brighton, PA

PREP: 20 min. • **COOK:** 2½ hours + standing • **MAKES:** 8 servings

- 1 Tbsp. canola oil
- 1 beef eye round roast (about 2½ lbs.)
- 1 garlic clove, minced
- 2 tsp. dried basil
- 1 tsp. salt
- 1 tsp. dried rosemary, crushed
- ½ tsp. pepper
- 1 medium onion, chopped
- 1 tsp. beef bouillon granules
- 1 cup brewed coffee
- ¾ cup water

GRAVY
- ¼ cup all-purpose flour
- ¼ cup cold water

1. In a Dutch oven, heat oil over medium heat; brown roast on all sides. Remove from pan. Mix the garlic and seasonings; sprinkle over roast.
2. Add onion to same pan; cook and stir over medium heat until tender; stir in bouillon, coffee and ¾ cup water. Add roast; bring to a boil. Reduce heat; simmer, covered, until the meat is tender, about 2½ hours.
3. Remove roast from pan, reserving cooking juices. Tent with foil; let stand 10 minutes before slicing.
4. Mix flour and cold water until smooth; stir into cooking juices. Bring to a boil, stirring constantly. Cook and stir until thickened, 1-2 minutes. Serve with roast.
1 SERVING: 198 cal., 6g fat (2g sat. fat), 65mg chol., 453mg sod., 5g carb. (1g sugars, 1g fiber), 28g pro.
Meat & Potato Pot Roast: Prepare roast as directed in step 1. Simmer 1¾ hours. Cut 16 small red potatoes in half and 5 carrots into chunks. Quarter 2 onions. Add to Dutch oven; cover and simmer for 45 minutes or until meat and vegetables are tender. Remove meat and vegetables; keep warm. Make gravy as directed in step 4.

SHRIMP PAD THAI

You can make this yummy Thai classic in no time. Find fish sauce and chili garlic sauce in the Asian foods aisle of your grocery store.
—Elise Ray, Shawnee, KS

TAKES: 30 min. • **MAKES:** 4 servings

- 4 oz. uncooked thick rice noodles
- ½ lb. uncooked small shrimp, peeled and deveined
- 2 tsp. canola oil
- 1 large onion, chopped
- 1 garlic clove, minced
- 1 large egg, lightly beaten
- 3 cups coleslaw mix
- 4 green onions, thinly sliced
- ⅓ cup rice vinegar
- ¼ cup sugar
- 3 Tbsp. reduced-sodium soy sauce
- 2 Tbsp. fish sauce or additional reduced-sodium soy sauce
- 2 to 3 tsp. chili garlic sauce
- 2 Tbsp. chopped salted peanuts
  Chopped fresh cilantro leaves

1. Cook the rice noodles according to package directions.
2. In a large nonstick skillet or wok, stir-fry shrimp in oil until shrimp turn pink; remove and set aside. Add onion and garlic to the pan. Make a well in the center of the onion mixture; add egg. Stir-fry for 2-3 minutes or until egg is completely set. Add the coleslaw mix, green onions, vinegar, sugar, soy sauce, fish sauce, chili garlic sauce and peanuts; heat through. Return shrimp to the pan and heat through. Drain noodles; toss with shrimp mixture. Garnish with cilantro.

1¼ CUPS: 338 cal., 7g fat (1g sat. fat), 115mg chol., 1675mg sod., 52g carb. (23g sugars, 3g fiber), 17g pro.

INSPIRED BY;
P.F. CHANG'S
SHRIMP PAD THAI

FAVORITE BARBECUED CHICKEN

What better place to find a fantastic barbecue sauce than Texas, and that's where this one is from—it's my father-in-law's recipe. We've served it at many family reunions and think it's the best!
—Bobbie Morgan, Woodstock, GA

PREP: 15 min. • **GRILL:** 35 min. • **MAKES:** 12 servings

> 2 broiler/fryer chickens (3 to 4 lbs. each), cut into 8 pieces each
>   Salt and pepper
>
> BARBECUE SAUCE
> 2 Tbsp. canola oil
> 2 small onions, finely chopped
> 2 cups ketchup
> ¼ cup lemon juice
> 2 Tbsp. brown sugar
> 2 Tbsp. water
> 1 tsp. ground mustard
> ½ tsp. garlic powder
> ¼ tsp. pepper
> ⅛ tsp. salt
> ⅛ tsp. hot pepper sauce

1. Sprinkle chicken pieces with salt and pepper. Grill skin side down, uncovered, on a greased grill rack over medium heat for 20 minutes.
2. Meanwhile, in a small saucepan, make barbecue sauce by heating oil over medium heat. Add the onion; saute until tender. Stir in the remaining sauce ingredients and bring to a boil. Reduce the heat; simmer, uncovered, for 10 minutes.
3. Turn chicken; brush with barbecue sauce. Grill 15-25 minutes longer, brushing frequently with sauce, until a thermometer reads 165° when inserted in the breast and 170°-175° in the thigh.
1 SERVING: 370 cal., 19g fat (5g sat. fat), 104mg chol., 622mg sod., 15g carb. (14g sugars, 0 fiber), 33g pro.

MOM'S MEAT LOAF

My mother made the best meat loaf, and now I do, too. When I first met my husband, he wasn't a meat loaf kind of guy, but this recipe won him over!
—Michelle Beran, Claflin, KS

PREP: 15 min. • **BAKE:** 1 hour + standing • **MAKES:** 6 servings

- 2 large eggs, lightly beaten
- ¾ cup 2% milk
- ⅔ cup finely crushed saltines
- ½ cup chopped onion
- 1 tsp. salt
- ½ tsp. rubbed sage
- Dash pepper
- 1½ lbs. lean ground beef (90% lean)
- 1 cup ketchup
- ½ cup packed brown sugar
- 1 tsp. Worcestershire sauce

1. Preheat oven to 350°. In a large bowl, combine the first 7 ingredients. Add beef; mix lightly but thoroughly. Shape into an 8x4-in. loaf in an ungreased 15x10x1-in. baking pan.
2. In a small bowl, combine remaining ingredients, stirring to dissolve sugar; remove ½ cup for sauce. Spread remaining mixture over meat loaf.
3. Bake 60-65 minutes or until a thermometer reads 160°. Let stand 10 minutes before slicing. Serve with reserved sauce.

1 SLICE: 366 cal., 12g fat (5g sat. fat), 135mg chol., 1092mg sod., 38g carb. (31g sugars, 0 fiber), 26g pro.

INSPIRED BY:
BOSTON MARKET'S MEATLOAF

HAVE IT YOUR WAY

For a tender meat loaf, use a gentle touch when mixing and shaping. Also, be sure to moisten the cracker crumbs or bread crumbs before adding them to the meat.

Feel free to swap ground turkey for the beef. It pairs perfectly with the earthy rubbed sage. Short on time? Skip the homemade sauce and use your favorite prepared barbecue sauce instead.

QUICK COCONUT SHRIMP

These coconut-fried shrimp are downright addicting. If you ask me, the bigger the shrimp, the better. That way you can pick up even more of that sweet pina colada sauce.
—Debra Barate, Seward, PA

TAKES: 20 min. • **MAKES:** 4 servings

- 1 lb. uncooked jumbo shrimp (about 12), peeled and deveined
- ¼ cup all-purpose flour
- 2 large egg whites, lightly beaten
- 1⅓ cups sweetened shredded coconut
  Oil for deep-fat frying
- 1 jar (12 oz.) pineapple preserves
- 1 Tbsp. frozen nonalcoholic pina colada mix, thawed

1. Starting with the tail, make a slit down the inner curve of each shrimp; press lightly to flatten. In three separate shallow bowls, place the flour, egg whites and coconut. Coat the shrimp with flour; dip into egg whites, then coat with the coconut.
2. In an electric skillet or deep-fat fryer, heat oil to 375°. Fry shrimp, a few at a time, for 1-1½ minutes on each side or until golden brown. Drain on paper towels.
3. In a small bowl, combine the preserves and pina colada mix. Serve with shrimp.
3 SHRIMP: 611 cal., 24g fat (11g sat. fat), 136mg chol., 244mg sod., 79g carb. (67g sugars, 0 fiber), 22g pro.

COUNTRY HAM & POTATOES

Here's a homestyle meal that's delicious for breakfast or dinner. The potatoes cook in the meat's drippings, which yield tender spuds with a tantalizing smoky ham flavor.
—Helen Bridges, Washington, VA

TAKES: 30 min. • **MAKES:** 6 servings

- 2   lbs. fully cooked sliced ham (about ½ in. thick)
- 2   to 3 Tbsp. butter
- 1½ lbs. potatoes, peeled, quartered and cooked
     Snipped fresh parsley

In a large heavy skillet, brown ham over medium-high heat in butter on both sides until heated through. Move ham to one side of the skillet; brown potatoes in drippings until tender. Sprinkle potatoes with parsley.

5 OZ.: 261 cal., 9g fat (5g sat. fat), 64mg chol., 1337mg sod., 21g carb. (1g sugars, 1g fiber), 28g pro.

INSPIRED BY:
CRACKER BARREL'S
HICKORY-SMOKED
COUNTRY HAM

GRILLED RIBEYE WITH GARLIC BLUE CHEESE MUSTARD SAUCE

This simple steak gets a big flavor boost from two of my favorites: mustard and blue cheese. My husband and I make this recipe to celebrate our anniversary each year!
—Ashley Lecker, Green Bay, WI

PREP: 20 min. • **GRILL:** 10 min. + standing • **MAKES:** 4 servings

- 1 cup half-and-half cream
- ½ cup Dijon mustard
- ¼ cup plus 2 tsp. crumbled blue cheese, divided
- 1 garlic clove, minced
- 2 beef ribeye steaks (1½ in. thick and 12 oz. each)
- 1 Tbsp. olive oil
- ¼ tsp. salt
- ¼ tsp. pepper

1. In a small saucepan over medium heat, whisk together cream, mustard, ¼ cup blue cheese and garlic. Bring to a simmer. Reduce heat to low; whisk occasionally.
2. Meanwhile, rub meat with olive oil; sprinkle with salt and pepper. Grill steaks, covered, on a greased rack over high direct heat for 4-6 minutes on each side until meat reaches desired doneness (for medium-rare, a thermometer should read 135°; medium, 140°; medium-well, 145°). Remove from grill; let stand 10 minutes while sauce finishes cooking. When sauce is reduced by half, pour over steaks; top with remaining blue cheese.

½ STEAK WITH 3 TBSP. SAUCE: 547 cal., 39g fat (17g sat. fat), 138mg chol., 1088mg sod., 3g carb. (2g sugars, 0 fiber), 34g pro.

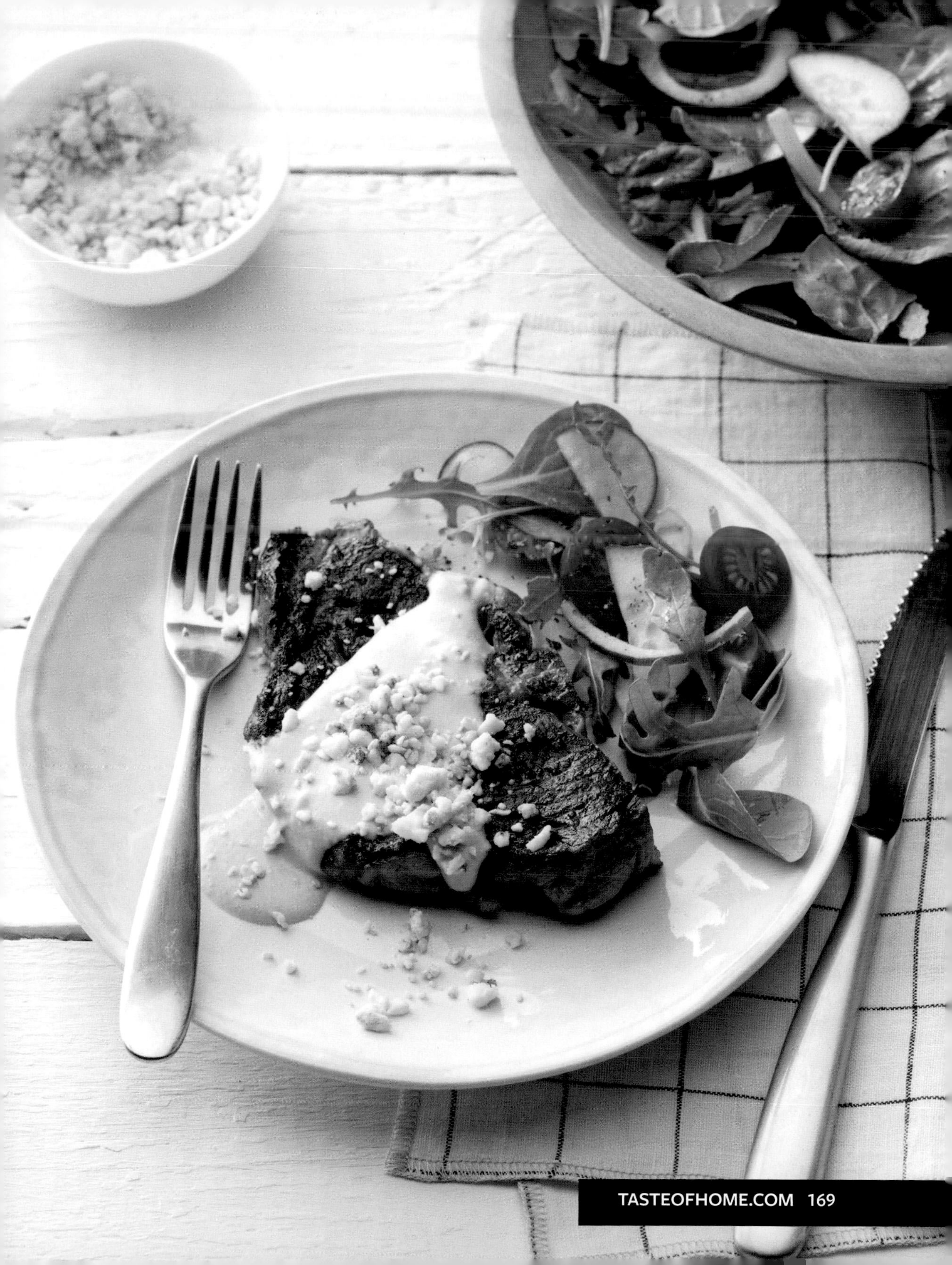

FANTASTIC FISH TACOS

Here's my crispy, crunchy take on fish tacos. They're always a hit with family and friends, and I like that they're a healthy alternative to fish that's deep-fried.

—Jennifer Palmer, Rancho Cucamonga, CA

TAKES: 30 min. • **MAKES:** 4 servings

- ½ cup fat-free mayonnaise
- 1 Tbsp. lime juice
- 2 tsp. fat-free milk
- 1 large egg
- 1 tsp. water
- ⅓ cup dry bread crumbs
- 2 Tbsp. salt-free lemon-pepper seasoning
- 1 lb. mahi mahi or cod fillets, cut into 1-in. strips
- 4 corn tortillas (6 in.), warmed

TOPPINGS
- 1 cup coleslaw mix
- 2 medium tomatoes, chopped
- 1 cup shredded reduced-fat Mexican cheese blend
- 1 Tbsp. minced fresh cilantro

1. For sauce, in a small bowl, mix mayonnaise, lime juice and milk; refrigerate until serving.

2. In a shallow bowl, whisk together egg and water. In another shallow bowl, toss bread crumbs with lemon pepper. Dip the fish fillets in egg mixture, then in crumb mixture, patting to help the coating adhere.

3. Place a large nonstick skillet over medium-high heat. Add fish; cook 2-4 minutes per side or until golden brown and fish just begins to flake easily with a fork. Serve in tortillas with toppings and sauce.

1 TACO: 321 cal., 10g fat (5g sat. fat), 148mg chol., 632mg sod., 29g carb. (5g sugars, 4g fiber), 34g pro.
DIABETIC EXCHANGES: 4 lean meat, 2 starch.

SIMPLE SESAME CHICKEN WITH COUSCOUS

I created this dish after my three kids tried Chinese takeout and asked for more. To make things easy, I often use a rotisserie chicken from the deli.
—Naylet LaRochelle, Miami, FL

TAKES: 25 min. • **MAKES:** 4 servings

1½ cups water
1 cup uncooked whole wheat couscous
1 Tbsp. olive oil
2 cups coleslaw mix
4 green onions, sliced
2 Tbsp. plus ½ cup reduced-fat Asian toasted sesame salad dressing, divided
2 cups shredded cooked chicken breast
2 Tbsp. minced fresh cilantro
Chopped peanuts, optional

1. In a small saucepan, bring water to a boil. Stir in the couscous. Remove from heat; let stand, covered, 5-10 minutes or until water is absorbed. Fluff with a fork.
2. In a large nonstick skillet, heat oil over medium heat. Add coleslaw mix; cook and stir 3-4 minutes or just until tender. Add the green onions, 2 Tbsp. dressing and couscous; heat through. Remove the couscous from pan; keep warm.
3. In same skillet, add chicken and remaining dressing; cook and stir over medium heat until heated through. Serve over couscous; top with cilantro and, if desired, peanuts.

1 CUP COUSCOUS WITH ½ CUP CHICKEN MIXTURE: 320 cal., 9g fat (1g sat. fat), 54mg chol., 442mg sod., 35g carb. (9g sugars, 5g fiber), 26g pro.
DIABETIC EXCHANGES: 3 lean meat, 2 starch, 1 fat.

WISCONSIN BUTTER-BASTED BURGERS

It's no secret that Wisconsinites love their dairy—in fact, they love it so much they top their burgers with a generous pat of butter. My recipe is a lot like the butter burgers you'll find in restaurants all over the state.

—Becky Carver, North Royalton, OH

TAKES: 30 min. • **MAKES:** 4 servings

- 1 lb. lean ground beef (90% lean)
- ½ tsp. seasoned salt
- ½ tsp. pepper
- ½ lb. fresh mushrooms
- 2 Tbsp. plus 4 tsp. butter, divided
- 4 hamburger buns, split
   Optional toppings: Tomato slices, lettuce leaves, dill pickle slices, ketchup and mustard

1. Sprinkle ground beef with seasoned salt and pepper. Pulse mushrooms in a food processor until finely chopped. Add to seasoned beef, mixing lightly but thoroughly. Shape into four ½-in.-thick patties.

2. In a large skillet, heat 2 Tbsp. butter over medium heat. Add burgers; cook 6-8 minutes on each side, basting with butter, until a thermometer reads 160°. Remove from heat; keep warm. Add bun tops to skillet; toast until golden brown.

3. Transfer burgers to bun bottoms. Top each with 1 tsp. butter. Replace bun tops. Serve with toppings.

1 BURGER: 400 cal., 21g fat (10g sat. fat), 96mg chol., 543mg sod., 24g carb. (3g sugars, 1g fiber), 28g pro.

INSPIRED BY:
CULVER'S
BUTTERBURGER "THE ORIGINAL"

SLOW-COOKER BARBACOA

My husband adores this roast simmered In lime juice, chipotle and cumin. I serve it over rice flavored with cilantro and more zippy lime.
—Aundrea McCormick, Denver, CO

PREP: 45 min. • **COOK:** 7 hours • **MAKES:** 8 servings

- ¼ cup lime juice
- ¼ cup cider vinegar
- 3 chipotle peppers in adobo sauce
- 4 garlic cloves, thinly sliced
- 4 tsp. ground cumin
- 3 tsp. dried oregano
- 1½ tsp. pepper
- ¾ tsp. salt
- ½ tsp. ground cloves
- 1 cup reduced-sodium chicken broth
- 1 boneless beef chuck roast (3 to 4 lbs.)
- 3 bay leaves

RICE
- 3 cups water
- 2 cups uncooked jasmine rice, rinsed and drained
- 3 Tbsp. butter
- 1½ tsp. salt
- ½ cup minced fresh cilantro
- 2 Tbsp. lime juice

1. Place the first 9 ingredients in a blender; cover and process until smooth. Add broth; pulse to combine.
2. Place roast and bay leaves in a 4- or 5-qt. slow cooker; pour sauce over top. Cook, covered, on low until meat is tender, 7-9 hours.
3. Prepare rice about 30 minutes before serving. In a large saucepan, combine water, rice, butter and salt; bring to a boil. Reduce heat; simmer, covered, until the liquid is absorbed and the rice is tender, 12-15 minutes. Remove from heat; gently stir in the minced cilantro and lime juice.
4. Remove roast from slow cooker; cool slightly. Discard bay leaves and skim fat from cooking juices. Shred beef with 2 forks; return to slow cooker. Serve with rice.

½ CUP BEEF MIXTURE WITH ⅔ CUP COOKED RICE: 513 cal., 21g fat (9g sat. fat), 122mg chol., 882mg sod., 40g carb. (1g sugars, 1g fiber), 37g pro.

INSPIRED BY:
ROCK BOTTOM RESTAURANT
& BREWERY'S
BACON CHEDDAR BURGER

BBQ BACON BURGER

Every family has a burger of choice, and this is ours. It's stacked tall with bacon and crunchy onion rings.
—Paula Homer, Nampa, ID

TAKES: 30 min. • **MAKES:** 6 servings

- 12 **frozen onion rings**
- 2 **lbs. ground beef**
- ¼ **tsp. garlic salt**
- ¼ **tsp. pepper**
- 6 **slices pepper jack cheese**
- 6 **hamburger buns, split and toasted**
- 1 **cup barbecue sauce**
- 6 **cooked bacon strips**
   Optional toppings: Lettuce leaves, sliced tomato and dill pickles

1. Bake onion rings according to package directions. Meanwhile, in a large bowl, combine beef, garlic salt and pepper; mix lightly but thoroughly. Shape into six ¾-in.-thick patties.
2. In a large nonstick skillet, cook burgers over medium heat 5-7 minutes on each side or until a thermometer reads 160°, adding cheese during the last minute of cooking. Serve on buns with barbecue sauce, bacon, onion rings and toppings as desired.
1 BURGER: 768 cal., 39g fat (15g sat. fat), 127mg chol., 1275mg sod., 60g carb. (18g sugars, 2g fiber), 42g pro.

GARLIC LEMON SHRIMP

This shrimp dish is amazingly quick to prepare. Serve it with crusty bread so you can soak up the luscious garlic lemon sauce.
—Athena Russell, Greenville, SC

TAKES: 20 min. • **MAKES:** 4 servings

- 2 Tbsp. olive oil
- 1 lb. uncooked shrimp (26-30 per lb.), peeled and deveined
- 3 garlic cloves, thinly sliced
- 1 Tbsp. lemon juice
- 1 tsp. ground cumin
- ¼ tsp. salt
- 2 Tbsp. minced fresh parsley
  Hot cooked pasta or rice

In a large skillet, heat oil over medium-high heat; saute shrimp for 3 minutes. Add garlic, lemon juice, cumin and salt; cook and stir until shrimp turn pink. Stir in parsley. Serve with pasta.

1 SERVING: 163 cal., 0g fat (1g sat. fat), 138mg chol., 284mg sod., 2g carb. (0 sugars, 0 fiber), 19g pro.

DIABETIC EXCHANGES: 3 lean meat, 1½ fat.

HAVE IT YOUR WAY
Cook shrimp in olive oil instead of butter to slash about 3 grams of saturated fat per serving.

Popular Pizza & Pasta

FRIDAY NIGHT CALLS FOR PIZZA AND PASTA! HANG UP THE PHONE: THESE HEARTWARMING ITALIAN FAVES ARE BETTER THAN TAKEOUT.

BARBECUED CHICKEN
PIZZAS, P. 197
INSPIRED BY:
CALIFORNIA PIZZA KITCHEN'S
BBQ CHICKEN PIZZA

BEST SPAGHETTI & MEATBALLS

One evening, we had unexpected company. Since I had some of these meatballs left over in the freezer, I warmed them up as appetizers. Everyone raved! This classic recipe makes a big batch and is perfect for entertaining.
—Mary Lou Koskella, Prescott, AZ

PREP: 30 min. • **COOK:** 2 hours • **MAKES:** 16 servings

- 2 Tbsp. olive oil
- 1½ cups chopped onions
- 3 garlic cloves, minced
- 2 cans (12 oz. each) tomato paste
- 3 cups water
- 1 can (29 oz.) tomato sauce
- ⅓ cup minced fresh parsley
- 1 Tbsp. dried basil
- 2 tsp. salt
- ½ tsp. pepper

MEATBALLS

- 4 large eggs, lightly beaten
- 2 cups soft bread cubes (cut into ¼-in. pieces)
- 1½ cups whole milk
- 1 cup grated Parmesan cheese
- 3 garlic cloves, minced
- 2 tsp. salt
- ½ tsp. pepper
- 3 lbs. ground beef
- 2 Tbsp. canola oil
- 2 lbs. spaghetti, cooked

1. In a Dutch oven, heat olive oil over medium heat. Add onions; saute until softened. Add garlic; cook 1 minute longer. Stir in the tomato paste; cook 3-5 minutes. Add next 6 ingredients. Bring to a boil. Reduce heat; simmer, covered, for 50 minutes.
2. Combine the first 7 meatball ingredients. Add beef; mix lightly but thoroughly. Shape into 1½-in. balls.
3. In a large skillet, heat canola oil over medium heat. Add the meatballs; brown in batches until no longer pink. Drain. Add to sauce; bring to a boil. Reduce heat; simmer, covered, until flavors are blended, about 1 hour, stirring occasionally. Serve with hot cooked spaghetti.
1 SERVING: 519 cal., 18g fat (6g sat. fat), 106mg chol., 1043mg sod., 59g carb. (8g sugars, 4g fiber), 30g pro.

INSPIRED BY:
SPAGHETTI WAREH
SPAGHETTI AND M

HAVE IT YOUR WAY
Instead of frying, you can bake the meatballs at 400° on a rack over a rimmed baking sheet until golden brown, about 20 minutes.

WHITE CHEDDAR MAC & CHEESE

My mac and cheese is simple and has lots of flavor from the cheeses and ground chipotle chile. I use conchiglie pasta because its large openings allow more melted cheese to pool inside. Yum!
—Colleen Delawder, Herndon, VA

TAKES: 25 min. • **MAKES:** 8 servings

- 1 pkg. (16 oz.) small pasta shells
- ½ cup butter, cubed
- ½ cup all-purpose flour
- ½ tsp. onion powder
- ½ tsp. ground chipotle pepper
- ½ tsp. pepper
- ¼ tsp. salt
- 4 cups 2% milk
- 2 cups shredded sharp white cheddar cheese
- 2 cups shredded Manchego or additional white cheddar cheese

1. In a 6-qt. stockpot, cook pasta according to package directions. Drain; return to pot.
2. Meanwhile, in a large saucepan, melt butter over medium heat. Stir in flour and seasonings until smooth; gradually whisk in milk. Bring to a boil, stirring constantly; cook and stir until thickened, 6-8 minutes. Remove from heat; stir in cheeses until melted. Add to pasta; toss to coat.
1 CUP: 650 cal., 35g fat (22g sat. fat), 101mg chol., 607mg sod., 55g carb. (8g sugars, 2g fiber), 27g pro.

PEPPERONI PAN PIZZA

I've spent years trying to come up with the perfect pizza crust and sauce, and they're paired up in this recipe. I fix this crispy pizza for my family often, and it always satisfies my husband and three sons.
—Susan Lindahl, Alford, FL

INSPIRED BY:
CALIFORNIA PIZZA KITCHEN'S PEPPERONI PIZZA

PREP: 30 min. • **BAKE:** 10 min. • **MAKES:** 2 pizzas (4 servings each)

- 2¾ to 3 cups all-purpose flour
- 1 pkg. (¼ oz.) active dry yeast
- ¼ tsp. salt
- 1 cup warm water (120° to 130°)
- 1 Tbsp. canola oil

SAUCE

- 1 can (14½ oz.) diced tomatoes, undrained
- 1 can (6 oz.) tomato paste
- 1 Tbsp. canola oil
- 1 tsp. salt
- ½ tsp. each dried basil, oregano, marjoram and thyme
- ¼ tsp. garlic powder
- ¼ tsp. pepper

PIZZAS

- 1 pkg. (3½ oz.) sliced pepperoni
- 5 cups shredded part-skim mozzarella cheese
- ¼ cup grated Parmesan cheese
- ¼ cup grated Romano cheese

1. In a large bowl, combine 2 cups flour, yeast and salt. Add water and oil; beat until smooth. Add enough remaining flour to form a soft dough.

2. Turn onto a floured surface; knead until smooth and elastic, 5-7 minutes. Cover and let stand for 10 minutes. Meanwhile, in a small bowl, combine tomatoes, tomato paste, oil and seasonings.

3. Divide dough in half; press into two 15x10x1-in. baking pans coated with cooking spray. Prick dough generously with a fork. Bake at 425° for 12-16 minutes or until lightly browned.

4. Spread sauce over crusts; top with pepperoni and cheeses. Bake for 8-10 minutes or until cheese is melted. Cut into squares.

FREEZE OPTION: Bake crusts and assemble pizzas as directed. Securely wrap and freeze unbaked pizzas. To use, unwrap pizzas; bake as directed, increasing time as necessary.

1 SERVING: 431 cal., 20g fat (10g sat. fat), 51mg chol., 985mg sod., 38g carb. (7g sugars, 3g fiber), 25g pro.

QUICK CARBONARA

Carbonara is a dinnertime classic, but my version cuts down on the time it takes to make. Loaded up with ham, bacon, olives, garlic and Parmesan, it certainly doesn't skimp on flavor.
—Carole Martin, Tallahassee, FL

TAKES: 30 min. • **MAKES:** 6 servings

- 12 oz. uncooked spaghetti
- 3 Tbsp. butter
- 3 Tbsp. canola oil
- 2 garlic cloves, minced
- 3 cups cubed fully cooked ham
- 8 bacon strips, cooked and crumbled
- 2 Tbsp. minced fresh parsley
- ¾ cup sliced ripe or pimiento-stuffed olives
- ½ cup grated Parmesan cheese

1. Cook spaghetti according to package directions; drain.
2. In a large skillet, heat butter and oil over medium heat; saute garlic 1 minute. Stir in ham and bacon; heat through. Add spaghetti and parsley; toss to combine.
3. Remove from heat. Stir in olives and cheese.
1 SERVING: 513 cal., 24g fat (8g sat. fat), 73mg chol., 1333mg sod., 45g carb. (2g sugars, 2g fiber), 28g pro.

BIG KAHUNA PIZZA

A prebaked pizza crust and refrigerated barbecued pork make this tasty supper idea super fast and super easy. Cut into bite-sized pieces, it can double as a great last-minute appetizer, too.
—Joni Hilton, Rocklin, CA

TAKES: 30 min. • **MAKES:** 8 servings

- 1 prebaked 12-in. pizza crust
- 1 carton (16 oz.) refrigerated fully cooked barbecued shredded pork
- 1 can (20 oz.) pineapple chunks, drained
- ⅓ cup chopped red onion
- 2 cups shredded part-skim mozzarella cheese

1. Place pizza crust on an ungreased 12-in. pizza pan. Spread shredded pork over crust; top with pineapple and onion. Sprinkle with cheese.

2. Bake at 350° for 20-25 minutes or until cheese is melted.

1 SLICE: 343 cal., 10g fat (4g sat. fat), 33mg chol., 856mg sod., 45g carb. (20g sugars, 2g fiber), 19g pro.

SHRIMP SCAMPI

This shrimp scampi recipe looks impressive, but it's easy to prepare. Lemon and herbs enhance the shrimp, and bread crumbs add a pleasing crunch. Served over pasta, this main dish is pretty enough for company.

—Lori Packer, Omaha, NE

TAKES: 20 min. • **MAKES:** 4 servings

3   to 4 garlic cloves, minced
¼   cup butter, cubed
¼   cup olive oil
1   lb. uncooked medium shrimp, peeled and deveined
¼   cup lemon juice
½   tsp. pepper
¼   tsp. dried oregano
½   cup grated Parmesan cheese
¼   cup dry bread crumbs
¼   cup minced fresh parsley
     Hot cooked angel hair pasta

1. In a 10-in. ovenproof skillet, saute garlic in butter and oil until fragrant. Add the shrimp, lemon juice, pepper and oregano; cook and stir until shrimp turn pink. Sprinkle with cheese, bread crumbs and parsley.

2. Broil 6 in. from the heat for 2-3 minutes or until topping is golden brown. Serve with pasta.

1 CUP: 395 cal., 30g fat (11g sat. fat), 177mg chol., 420mg sod., 9g carb. (1g sugars, 1g fiber), 24g pro.

Grilled Shrimp Scampi: Omit the butter, oregano, Parmesan, bread crumbs and pasta. Substitute jumbo shrimp for the medium shrimp. In a large bowl, whisk the garlic, oil, lemon juice and pepper. Add the shrimp; toss to coat. Refrigerate, covered, 30 minutes. Thread the shrimp onto 4 metal or soaked wooden skewers. Grill, covered, over medium heat or broil 4 in. from heat 6-8 minutes or until shrimp turn pink, turning once. Serve with hot cooked rice; sprinkle with parsley.

Garlic Lemon Shrimp: Omit the butter, pepper, oregano, Parmesan and bread crumbs. In a large skillet, saute the shrimp in 2 Tbsp. oil for 3 minutes. Add the garlic, 1 Tbsp. lemon juice, 1 tsp. cumin and ¼ tsp. salt; cook and stir until shrimp turn pink. Stir in 2 Tbsp. minced fresh parsley. Serve with pasta.

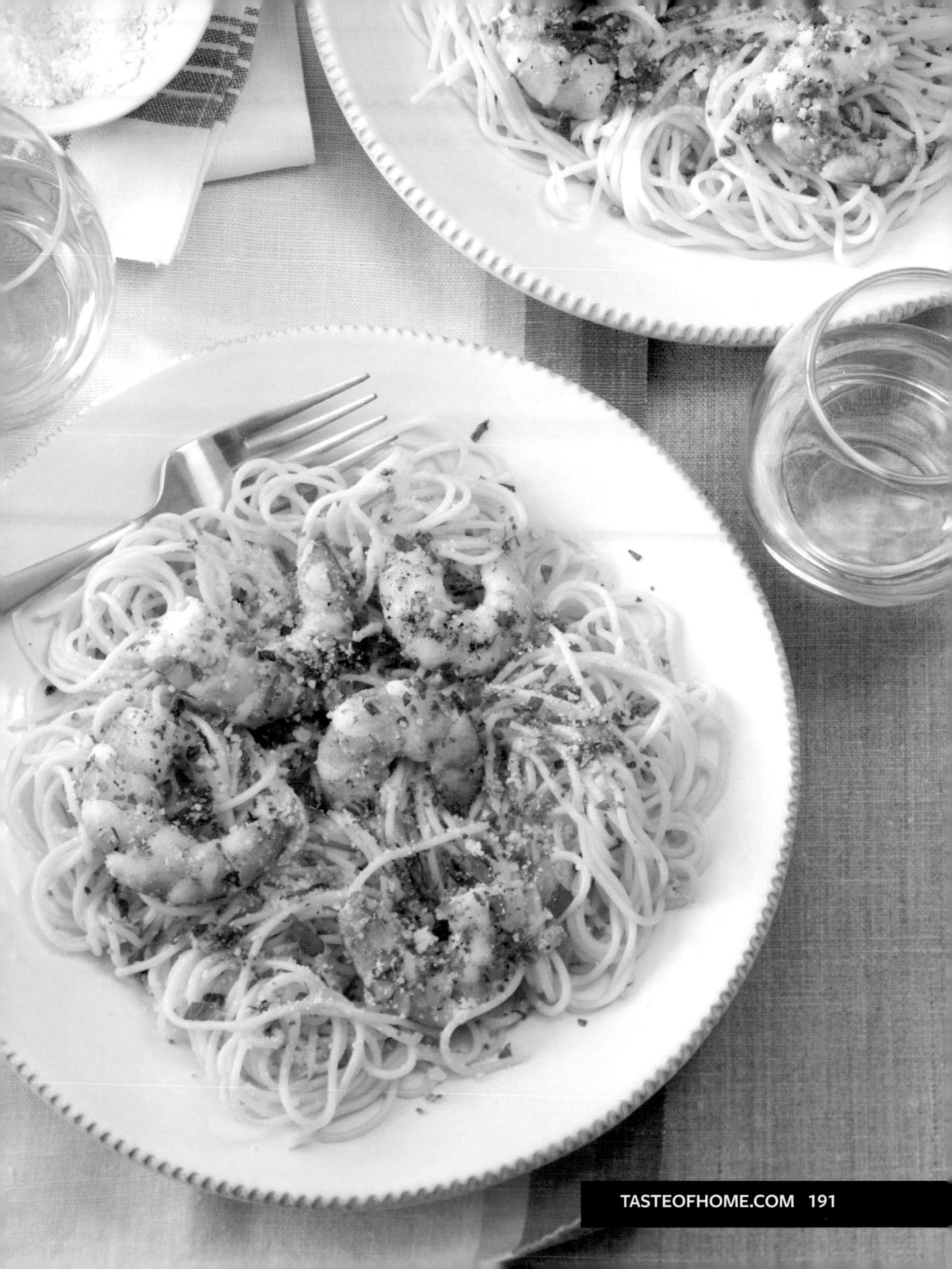

SAUCY THAI CHICKEN PIZZAS

Here's a fun riff on the popular peanut-flavored chicken served at Thai restaurants. This recipe takes it a step further and uses the chicken and sauce to make an extraordinary sweet and salty pizza.
—*Taste of Home* Test Kitchen

INSPIRED BY:
CALIFORNIA PIZZA KITCHEN'S
THAI CHICKEN PIZZA

PREP: 4¼ hours • **BAKE:** 10 min. • **MAKES:** 2 pizzas (6 slices each)

- 3   lbs. boneless skinless chicken thighs
- ¾   cup sugar
- ¾   cup reduced-sodium soy sauce
- ⅓   cup cider vinegar
- 1   garlic clove, minced
- ¾   tsp. ground ginger
- ¼   tsp. pepper
- 1   cup Thai peanut sauce
- 2   prebaked 12-in. pizza crusts
- 2   cups coleslaw mix
- 2   cups shredded part-skim mozzarella cheese
- 4   green onions, thinly sliced
- ½   cup chopped salted peanuts
- ¼   cup minced fresh cilantro

1. Place the chicken thighs in a 4- or 5-qt. slow cooker. In a small bowl, mix sugar, soy sauce, vinegar, garlic, ginger and pepper; pour over chicken. Cook, covered, on low 4-5 hours or until chicken is tender.

2. Preheat oven to 450°. Remove chicken from slow cooker; discard cooking juices. Shred chicken with 2 forks; transfer to large bowl. Add peanut sauce; toss to coat.

3. Place crusts on 2 ungreased 12-in. pizza pans or baking sheets. Spoon chicken mixture over crusts; top with coleslaw mix and cheese. Bake 10-12 minutes or until cheese is melted. Sprinkle with green onions, peanuts and cilantro.

1 SLICE: 522 cal., 23g fat (6g sat. fat), 88mg chol., 803mg sod., 40g carb. (9g sugars, 2g fiber), 37g pro.

FOUR-CHEESE CHICKEN FETTUCCINE

As a cattle rancher, my husband is a big fan of beef. But he always tells me he loves this chicken casserole! I first tasted it at a potluck, and now I fix it for my family once or twice a month.
—Rochelle Brownlee, Big Timber, MT

PREP: 20 min. • **BAKE:** 30 min. • **MAKES:** 8 servings

- 8   oz. uncooked fettuccine
- 1   can (10¾ oz.) condensed cream of mushroom soup, undiluted
- 1   pkg. (8 oz.) cream cheese, cubed
- 1   jar (4½ oz.) sliced mushrooms, drained
- 1   cup heavy whipping cream
- ½   cup butter
- ¼   tsp. garlic powder
- ¾   cup grated Parmesan cheese
- ½   cup shredded part-skim mozzarella cheese
- ½   cup shredded Swiss cheese
- 2½ cups cubed cooked chicken

TOPPING
- ⅓   cup seasoned bread crumbs
- 2   Tbsp. butter, melted
- 1   to 2 Tbsp. grated Parmesan cheese

1. Cook fettuccine according to package directions.

2. Meanwhile, in a large kettle, combine the soup, cream cheese, mushrooms, cream, butter and garlic powder. Stir in cheeses; cook and stir until melted. Add chicken; heat through. Drain fettuccine; add to the sauce.

3. Transfer to a shallow greased 2½-qt. baking dish. Combine topping ingredients; sprinkle over chicken mixture. Cover and bake at 350° for 25 minutes. Uncover; bake 5-10 minutes longer or until golden brown.

1 SERVING: 641 cal., 47g fat (27g sat. fat), 167mg chol., 895mg sod., 29g carb. (3g sugars, 2g fiber), 28g pro.

BARBECUED CHICKEN PIZZAS

So fast and so easy with refrigerated pizza crust, these saucy, smoky pizzas make quick fans with their hot-off-the-grill, rustic flavor. They're perfect for spur-of-the-moment cookouts and summer dinners on the patio.
—Alicia Trevithick, Temecula, CA

PREP: 25 min. • **GRILL:** 10 min. • **MAKES:** 2 pizzas (4 pieces each)

- 2 boneless skinless chicken breast halves (6 oz. each)
- ¼ tsp. pepper
- 1 cup barbecue sauce, divided
- 1 tube (13.8 oz.) refrigerated pizza crust
- 2 tsp. olive oil
- 2 cups shredded Gouda cheese
- 1 small red onion, halved and thinly sliced
- ¼ cup minced fresh cilantro

1. Sprinkle chicken with pepper; place on an oiled grill rack over medium heat. Grill, covered, until a thermometer reads 165°, 5-7 minutes per side, basting frequently with ½ cup barbecue sauce during the last 4 minutes. Cool slightly. Cut into cubes.
2. Divide dough in half. On a well-greased large sheet of heavy-duty foil, press each portion of dough into a 10x8-in. rectangle; brush lightly with oil. Invert dough onto grill rack; peel off foil. Grill, covered, over medium heat until bottom is lightly browned, 1-2 minutes.
3. Remove from grill. Spread grilled sides with remaining barbecue sauce. Top with cheese, chicken and onion. Grill, covered, until bottom is lightly browned and cheese is melted, 2-3 minutes. Sprinkle with cilantro.

1 PIECE: 339 cal., 12g fat (6g sat. fat), 56mg chol., 956mg sod., 39g carb. (15g sugars, 1g fiber), 20g pro.

INSPIRED BY:
NOODLES & COMPANY'S
PESTO CAVATAPPI

CHICKEN PESTO WITH PASTA

Keep a container of pesto in the freezer. The next time you have leftover chicken, whip up this simple pasta for lunch or dinner.
—*Taste of Home* Test Kitchen

TAKES: 20 min. • **MAKES:** 8 servings

- 1 pkg. (16 oz.) cellentani or spiral pasta
- 2 cups cubed rotisserie chicken
- 2 medium tomatoes, chopped
- 1 container (7 oz.) prepared pesto
- ¼ cup pine nuts, toasted

In a Dutch oven, cook pasta according to package directions; drain and return to pan. Stir in chicken, tomatoes and pesto; heat through. Sprinkle with pine nuts.

NOTE: To toast nuts, bake in a shallow pan in a 350° oven for 5-10 minutes or cook in a skillet over low heat until lightly browned, stirring occasionally.

1¼ CUPS: 404 cal., 16g fat (3g sat. fat), 31mg chol., 348mg sod., 46g carb. (4g sugars, 3g fiber), 20g pro.

SPINACH RAVIOLI BAKE

This entree is unbelievably simple to prepare yet tastes delicious. Using frozen ravioli—straight from the bag without cooking it first—saves so much time.

—Susan Kehl, Pembroke Pines, FL

PREP: 5 min. • **BAKE:** 40 min. • **MAKES:** 6 servings

- 2 cups spaghetti sauce
- 1 pkg. (25 oz.) frozen sausage ravioli or ravioli of your choice
- 2 cups shredded part-skim mozzarella cheese
- 1 pkg. (10 oz.) frozen chopped spinach, thawed and squeezed dry
- ¼ cup grated Parmesan cheese

1. Place 1 cup spaghetti sauce in a greased shallow 2-qt. baking dish. Top with half of the ravioli, mozzarella cheese, spinach and Parmesan cheese. Repeat layers.

2. Bake, uncovered, at 350° for 40-45 minutes or until heated through and cheese is melted.

1 CUP: 470 cal., 17g fat (7g sat. fat), 67mg chol., 1441mg sod., 54g carb. (7g sugars, 7g fiber), 27g pro.

INSPIRED BY:
THE OLD SPAGHETTI FACTORY'S SPINACH & CHEESE RAVIOLI

MEXICAN CHICKEN FAJITA PIZZA

This has always been a hit with my kids. And it's such a great way to sneak in extra vegetables.
—Carrie Shaub, Mount Joy, PA

TAKES: 30 min. • **MAKES:** 6 servings

- 1 pkg. (13.8 oz.) refrigerated pizza crust
- 8 oz. boneless skinless chicken breasts, cut into thin strips
- 1 tsp. canola oil, divided
- 1 medium onion, sliced
- 1 medium sweet red pepper, sliced
- 1 medium green pepper, sliced
- 1 tsp. chili powder
- ½ tsp. ground cumin
- 1 garlic clove, minced
- ¼ cup chunky salsa
- 2 cups shredded reduced-fat Mexican cheese blend
- 1 Tbsp. minced fresh cilantro
  Sour cream and additional salsa, optional

1. Unroll dough into a 15x10x1-in. baking pan coated with cooking spray; flatten dough and build up edges slightly. Bake at 425° for 8-10 minutes or until edges are lightly browned.

2. Meanwhile, in a large nonstick skillet coated with cooking spray, cook chicken over medium heat in ½ tsp. oil for 4-6 minutes or until no longer pink; remove and keep warm.

3. In the same pan, saute the onion, peppers, chili powder and cumin in remaining oil until crisp-tender. Add garlic; cook 1 minute longer. Stir in salsa and chicken.

4. Sprinkle half of the cheese over prepared crust; top with chicken mixture and remaining cheese. Bake for 8-10 minutes or until crust is golden brown and cheese is melted. Sprinkle with cilantro. Serve with sour cream and additional salsa if desired.

1 PIECE: 351 cal., 12g fat (4g sat. fat), 48mg chol., 767mg sod., 38g carb. (7g sugars, 2g fiber), 25g pro.
DIABETIC EXCHANGES: 3 lean meat, 2 starch, 1 vegetable, ½ fat.

BEST LASAGNA

If you're in need of a home run lasagna recipe, you can't go wrong with this deliciously rich and meaty version. My grown sons and daughter-in-law request it for their birthdays, too.
—Pam Thompson, Girard, IL

PREP: 1 hour • **BAKE:** 50 min. + standing • **MAKES:** 12 servings

9	lasagna noodles
1¼	lbs. bulk Italian sausage
¾	lb. ground beef
1	medium onion, diced
3	garlic cloves, minced
2	cans (one 28 oz., one 15 oz.) crushed tomatoes
2	cans (6 oz. each) tomato paste
⅔	cup water
2	to 3 Tbsp. sugar
3	Tbsp. plus ¼ cup minced fresh parsley, divided
2	tsp. dried basil
¾	tsp. fennel seed
¾	tsp. salt, divided
¼	tsp. coarsely ground pepper
1	large egg, lightly beaten
1	carton (15 oz.) ricotta cheese
4	cups shredded part-skim mozzarella cheese
¾	cup grated Parmesan cheese

1. Cook the noodles according to package directions; drain. Meanwhile, in a Dutch oven, cook sausage, beef and onion over medium heat 8-10 minutes or until the meat is no longer pink, breaking up meat into crumbles. Add garlic; cook 1 minute. Drain.
2. Stir in tomatoes, tomato paste, water, sugar, 3 Tbsp. parsley, basil, fennel, ½ tsp. salt and pepper; bring to a boil. Reduce heat; simmer, uncovered, 30 minutes, stirring occasionally.
3. In a small bowl, mix the egg, ricotta cheese, and remaining parsley and salt.
4. Preheat oven to 375°. Spread 2 cups meat sauce into an ungreased 13x9-in. baking dish. Layer with 3 noodles and a third of the ricotta mixture. Sprinkle with 1 cup mozzarella cheese and 2 Tbsp. Parmesan cheese. Repeat layers twice. Top with remaining meat sauce and cheeses (dish will be full).
5. Bake, covered, 25 minutes. Bake, uncovered, 25 minutes longer or until bubbly. Let stand 15 minutes before serving.
1 PIECE: 519 cal., 27g fat (13g sat. fat), 109mg chol., 1013mg sod., 35g carb. (10g sugars, 4g fiber), 35g pro.

INSPIRED BY:
CARRABBA'S ITALIA
LASAGNE

HAVE IT YOUR WAY
Don't have Italian sausage on hand? Ground beef will work just fine. If you want to add veggies, saute them ahead of time to release some extra moisture. Then layer in the vegetables with your meat and cheeses.

Favorite Odds & Ends

FROM SHAKES AND FRIES TO BREADS AND SIDES, THESE DOUBLE-TAKE RECIPES ROUND OUT HOMEMADE MENUS WITH FAMILIAR FLAIR.

THIN MINT MILK SHAKE, P. 224
INSPIRED BY: MCDONALD'S
SHAMROCK SHAKE

CHEESE FRIES

I came up with this recipe after my daughter had cheese fries at a restaurant and couldn't stop talking about them. She loves that I can fix them so quickly at home.
—Melissa Tatum, Greensboro, NC

TAKES: 20 min. • **MAKES:** 8 servings

- 1 **pkg. (28 oz.) frozen steak fries**
- 1 **can (10¾ oz.) condensed cheddar cheese soup, undiluted**
- ¼ **cup 2% milk**
- ½ **tsp. garlic powder**
- ¼ **tsp. onion powder**
  Paprika

1. Arrange steak fries in a single layer in 2 greased 15x10x1-in. baking pans. Bake at 450° for 15-18 minutes or until tender and golden brown.
2. Meanwhile, in a small saucepan, combine the soup, milk, garlic powder and onion powder; heat through. Drizzle over fries; sprinkle with paprika.

1 SERVING: 166 cal., 5g fat (2g sat. fat), 2mg chol., 657mg sod., 27g carb. (3g sugars, 3g fiber), 3g pro.
DIABETIC EXCHANGES: 1 starch, 1 fat.

INSPIRED BY:
SHAKE SHACK'S
CHEESE FRIES

INSPIRED BY:
POPEYE'S
BISCUITS

SOUTHERN BUTTERMILK BISCUITS

The recipe for these biscuits has been handed down for many generations. They're simple to make and smell so good when baking.
—Fran Thompson, Tarboro, NC

TAKES: 30 min. • **MAKES:** 8 biscuits

½ cup cold butter, cubed
2 cups self-rising flour
¾ cup buttermilk
  Melted butter

1. In a large bowl, cut butter into flour until mixture resembles coarse crumbs. Stir in buttermilk just until moistened. Turn onto a lightly floured surface; knead 3-4 times. Pat or lightly roll to ¾-in. thickness. Cut with a floured 2½-in. biscuit cutter.
2. Place on a greased baking sheet. Bake at 425° until golden brown, 11-13 minutes. Brush tops with butter. Serve warm.
NOTE: As a substitute for each cup of self-rising flour, place 1½ tsp. baking powder and ½ tsp. salt in a measuring cup. Add all-purpose flour to measure 1 cup.
1 BISCUIT: 197 cal., 11 g fat (7 g sat. fat), 28 mg chol., 451 mg sod., 22 g carb., 1 g fiber, 4 g pro.

MEXICAN STREET CORN BAKE

We discovered Mexican street corn at a festival. This easy one-pan version saves on prep and cleanup. Every August, I freeze some of our own fresh sweet corn and use that in this recipe, but store-bought corn works just as well.
—Erin Wright, Wallace, KS

PREP: 10 min. • **BAKE:** 35 min. • **MAKES:** 6 servings

- 6 cups frozen corn (about 30 oz.), thawed and drained
- 1 cup mayonnaise
- 1 tsp. ground chipotle pepper
- ¼ tsp. salt
- ¼ tsp. pepper
- 6 Tbsp. chopped green onions, divided
- ½ cup grated Parmesan cheese
  Lime wedges, optional

1. Preheat oven to 350°. Mix first 5 ingredients and 4 Tbsp. green onions; transfer to a greased 1½-qt. baking dish. Sprinkle with Parmesan cheese.
2. Bake, covered, 20 minutes. Uncover; bake until bubbly and lightly browned, 15-20 minutes. Sprinkle with remaining green onions. If desired, serve with lime wedges.

⅔ CUP: 391 cal., 30g fat (5g sat. fat), 8mg chol., 423mg sod., 30g carb. (4g sugars, 3g fiber), 6g pro.

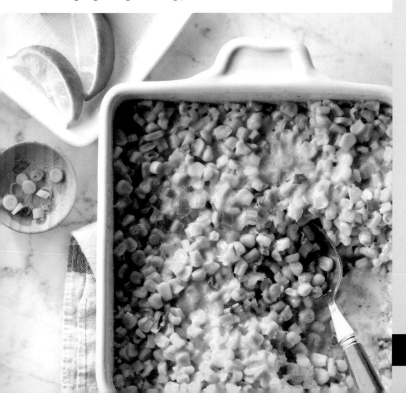

ROSEMARY ORANGE BREAD

Rosemary is my favorite herb. This bread pairs well with a roast or pasta. It's especially festive to serve at holiday time.
—Deidre Fallavollita, Vienna, VA

PREP: 20 min. + rising • **BAKE:** 45 min. + cooling
MAKES: 1 loaf (16 slices)

- 1 pkg. (¼ oz.) active dry yeast
- ¾ cup warm water (110° to 115°)
- ¾ cup orange juice
- 2 Tbsp. honey
- 1 Tbsp. vegetable oil
- 1 Tbsp. minced fresh rosemary or 1 tsp. dried rosemary, crushed
- 2 tsp. salt
- 1 tsp. grated orange zest
- 3¾ to 4½ cups all-purpose flour
- 1 large egg white
  Additional fresh rosemary and whole peppercorns, optional

1. In a large bowl, dissolve yeast in warm water. Add orange juice, honey, oil, rosemary, salt, orange zest and 2 cups flour; beat until smooth. Stir in enough remaining flour to form a soft dough.
2. Turn onto a floured surface; knead until smooth and elastic, 6-8 minutes. Place in a greased bowl, turning once to grease top. Cover and let rise in a warm place until doubled, about 1 hour.
3. Punch dough down. Roll into a 15x1-in. rectangle. Starting at a short end, roll up jelly-roll style. Pinch edges to seal and shape into an oval. Place seam side down on a greased baking sheet. Cover and let rise until nearly doubled, about 30 minutes.
4. Bake at 375° for 20 minutes. Whisk egg white; brush over loaf. Place small sprigs of rosemary and peppercorns on top if desired. Bake 25 minutes longer or until browned. Remove from pan to wire rack to cool.
1 SLICE: 130 cal., 1g fat (0 sat. fat), 0 chol., 299mg sod., 26g carb. (4g sugars, 1g fiber), 3g pro.

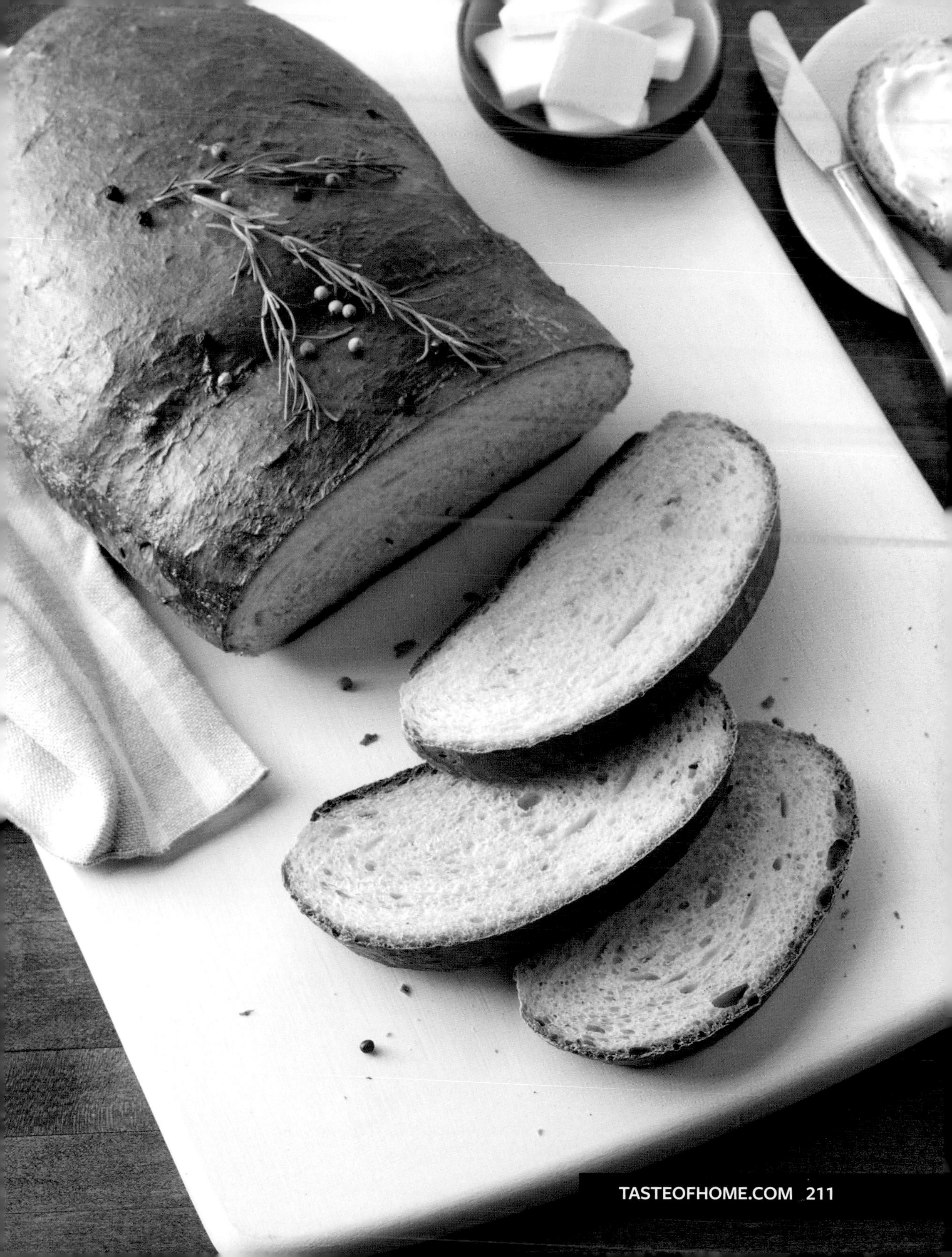

BEEF-STUFFED POTATOES

Here's a stuffed potato with a twist. The combo of green chiles and cheese is always popular with teenagers.

—Kay Scheidler, Bull Shoals, AR

PREP: 20 min. • **BAKE:** 70 min. • **MAKES:** 6 servings

- 6 medium baking potatoes
- 1 lb. ground beef
- 2 Tbsp. chopped onion
- ⅓ cup sour cream
- 1 can (4 oz.) chopped green chiles
- 3 Tbsp. butter
- 1 Tbsp. Worcestershire sauce
- 1 tsp. salt
- ½ tsp. garlic powder
- ½ tsp. chili powder
- ¾ cup shredded cheddar cheese

1. Bake potatoes at 375° for 1 hour or until tender. Cool. Meanwhile, in a large skillet, cook the beef and onion over medium heat until the meat is no longer pink; drain.
2. Cut a thin slice off the top of each potato. Carefully scoop out pulp, leaving a thin shell; place pulp in a bowl. Add sour cream, chiles, butter, Worcestershire sauce, salt, garlic powder and chili powder; mash or beat. Stir in meat mixture until combined. Stuff into potato shells.
3. Place on an ungreased baking sheet. Sprinkle with cheese. Bake at 350° for 10-15 minutes or until heated through.

1 SERVING: 422 cal., 19g fat (11g sat. fat), 76mg chol., 711mg sod., 41g carb. (4g sugars, 4g fiber), 21g pro.

INSPIRED BY:
MCALISTER'S DELI
SPUD OLE

MAKEOVER CHEDDAR BISCUITS

These biscuits have a cheesy richness everyone loves. I serve them with steaming bowls of chili or a hearty beef soup.
—Alicia Rooker, Milwaukee, WI

TAKES: 30 min. • **MAKES:** 15 biscuits

- 1 cup all-purpose flour
- 1 cup cake flour
- 1½ tsp. baking powder
- ¾ tsp. salt
- ½ tsp. garlic powder, divided
- ¼ tsp. baking soda
- 4 Tbsp. cold butter, divided
- ⅓ cup finely shredded cheddar cheese
- 1 cup buttermilk
- ½ tsp. dried parsley flakes

1. In a large bowl, combine the flours, baking powder, salt, ¼ tsp. garlic powder and baking soda. Cut in 3 Tbsp. butter until mixture resembles coarse crumbs; add cheese. Stir in buttermilk just until moistened.
2. Drop by 2 tablespoonfuls 2 in. apart onto baking sheets coated with cooking spray. Bake at 425° for 10-12 minutes or until golden brown. Melt remaining butter; stir in parsley and remaining garlic powder. Brush over biscuits. Serve warm.
1 BISCUIT: 106 cal., 4g fat (3g sat. fat), 11mg chol., 233mg sod., 14g carb. (1g sugars, 0 fiber), 3g pro.

ROASTED ROOT VEGETABLES

Pleasantly seasoned with rosemary and garlic, this appealing side dish showcases good-for-you turnips, carrots and potatoes. It's a nice addition to any meal, especially on holidays.
—Kerry Sullivan, Longwood, FL

PREP: 15 min. • **BAKE:** 45 min. • **MAKES:** 12 servings

- 5 medium red potatoes, cubed
- 4 medium carrots, cut into ½-in. slices
- 2 small turnips, peeled and cubed
- 1 garlic clove, minced
- 2 to 4 Tbsp. olive oil
- 1 Tbsp. minced fresh rosemary or 1 tsp. dried rosemary, crushed
- ½ tsp. salt
- ¼ tsp. pepper

1. Place the potatoes, carrots, turnips and garlic in a greased 13x9-in. baking dish. Drizzle with oil; sprinkle with rosemary, salt and pepper. Stir to coat.

2. Bake, uncovered, at 350° for 35 minutes. Increase temperature to 450°; bake 10-15 minutes longer or until vegetables are tender.

¾ CUP: 55 cal., 3g fat (0 sat. fat), 0 chol., 144mg sod., 7g carb. (0 sugars, 2g fiber), 1g pro.
DIABETIC EXCHANGES: 1 vegetable, ½ fat.

TRIPLE CHEESE TWISTS

Our stovetop macaroni and cheese is extra special, thanks to the buttery crumb topping.
—*Taste of Home* Test Kitchen

TAKES: 25 min. • **MAKES:** 8 servings

- 1 pkg. (16 oz.) spiral pasta
- 1 small onion, chopped
- 1 garlic clove, minced
- 6 Tbsp. butter, divided
- 6 Tbsp. all-purpose flour
- 4 cups whole milk
- 1 can (14½ oz.) vegetable or chicken broth
- 1 cup shredded cheddar cheese
- 1 cup shredded Monterey Jack cheese
- ½ cup shredded Parmesan cheese
- ¼ cup bread crumbs
- ½ tsp. Italian seasoning

1. Cook pasta according to package directions. Meanwhile, in a large saucepan, saute onion and garlic in 4 Tbsp. butter until tender. Stir in the flour until blended. Gradually add milk and broth. Bring to a boil; cook and stir for 2 minutes or until thickened. Remove from the heat; stir in cheeses until melted.

2. Melt the remaining butter; stir in bread crumbs and Italian seasoning. Drain pasta; toss with cheese sauce. Sprinkle with seasoned bread crumbs.

1 CUP: 527 cal., 24g fat (15g sat. fat), 71mg chol., 644mg sod., 57g carb. (9g sugars, 2g fiber), 21g pro.

INSPIRED BY:
CHIPOTLE'S
CILANTRO-LIME RICE

CILANTRO-LIME RICE

I threw this together one night when I was making fajitas, and everyone loved it! It's an easy side dish and pairs well with grilled kabobs, too.
—Robin Baskette, Lexington, KY

TAKES: 20 min. • **MAKES:** 3 cups

- 1 cup uncooked jasmine rice
- 2 cups reduced-sodium chicken broth
- 2 Tbsp. lime juice
- 2 Tbsp. minced fresh cilantro
- ⅛ tsp. ground nutmeg

In a small saucepan, combine rice and broth; bring to a boil. Reduce heat; simmer, covered, until liquid is absorbed and rice is tender, 12-15 minutes. Add lime juice, cilantro and nutmeg; fluff with a fork.
½ CUP: 130 cal., 0 fat (0 sat. fat), 0 chol., 191mg sod., 28g carb. (0 sugars, 0 fiber), 4g pro.
DIABETIC EXCHANGES: 2 starch.

SAVORY BISCUIT-BREADSTICKS

I love to experiment in the kitchen with simple ingredients like refrigerated biscuits. The results usually are a big hit, like these super fast breadsticks.
—Billy Hensley, Mount Carmel, TN

TAKES: 20 min. • **MAKES:** 10 breadsticks

- ½ cup grated Parmesan cheese
- 2 tsp. dried minced garlic
- ¼ tsp. crushed red pepper flakes
- 1 tube (12 oz.) refrigerated buttermilk biscuits
- 2 Tbsp. olive oil

Preheat oven to 400°. In a shallow bowl, mix cheese, garlic and pepper flakes. Roll each biscuit into a 6-in. rope. Brush lightly with oil; roll in cheese mixture. Place on a greased baking sheet. Bake until golden brown, 8-10 minutes.

1 BREADSTICK. 142 cal., 8g fat (2g sat. fat), 3mg chol., 353mg sod., 16g carb. (2g sugars, 0 fiber), 3g pro.

INSPIRED BY:
OLIVE GARDEN'S BREADSTICKS

SWEET RASPBERRY TEA

You only need a handful of ingredients to stir together this bright and refreshing sipper. It's refreshing on a hot day.
—*Taste of Home* Test Kitchen

Prep: 10 min. • **Cook:** 15 min. + chilling • **Makes:** 15 servings

- 4 qt. water, divided
- 10 tea bags
- 1 pkg. (12 oz.) frozen unsweetened raspberries, thawed and undrained
- 1 cup sugar
- 3 Tbsp. lime juice

1. In a saucepan, bring 2 qt. water to a boil; remove from heat. Add tea bags; steep, covered, 5-8 minutes according to taste. Discard tea bags.
2. Place raspberries, sugar and remaining water in a large saucepan; bring to a boil, stirring to dissolve sugar. Reduce heat; simmer, uncovered, 3 minutes. Press mixture through a fine-mesh strainer into a bowl; discard pulp and seeds.
3. In a large pitcher, combine tea, raspberry syrup and lime juice. Refrigerate, covered, until cold.

1 CUP: 63 cal., 0 fat (0 sat. fat), 0 chol., 0 sod., 16g carb. (15g sugars, 1g fiber), 0 pro.

SUPER QUICK CHICKEN FRIED RICE

After my first child was born, I needed meals that were satisfying and fast. This fried rice is now part of our regular dinner rotation.
—Alicia Gower, Auburn, NY

Takes: 30 min. • **Makes:** 6 servings

- 1 pkg. (12 oz.) frozen mixed vegetables
- 2 Tbsp. olive oil, divided
- 2 large eggs, lightly beaten
- 4 Tbsp. sesame oil, divided
- 3 pkg. (8.8 oz. each) ready-to-serve garden vegetable rice
- 1 rotisserie chicken, skin removed, shredded
- ¼ tsp. salt
- ¼ tsp. pepper

1. Prepare frozen vegetables according to package directions. Meanwhile, in a large skillet, heat 1 Tbsp. olive oil over medium-high heat. Pour in eggs; cook and stir until eggs are thickened and no liquid egg remains. Remove from pan.
2. In same skillet, heat 2 Tbsp. sesame oil and remaining olive oil over medium-high heat. Add rice; cook and stir until rice begins to brown, 10-12 minutes.
3. Stir in chicken, salt and pepper. Add eggs and vegetables; heat through, breaking eggs into small pieces and stirring to combine. Drizzle with remaining sesame oil.
1½ CUPS: 548 cal., 25g fat (5g sat. fat), 163mg chol., 934mg sod., 43g carb. (3g sugars, 3g fiber), 38g pro.

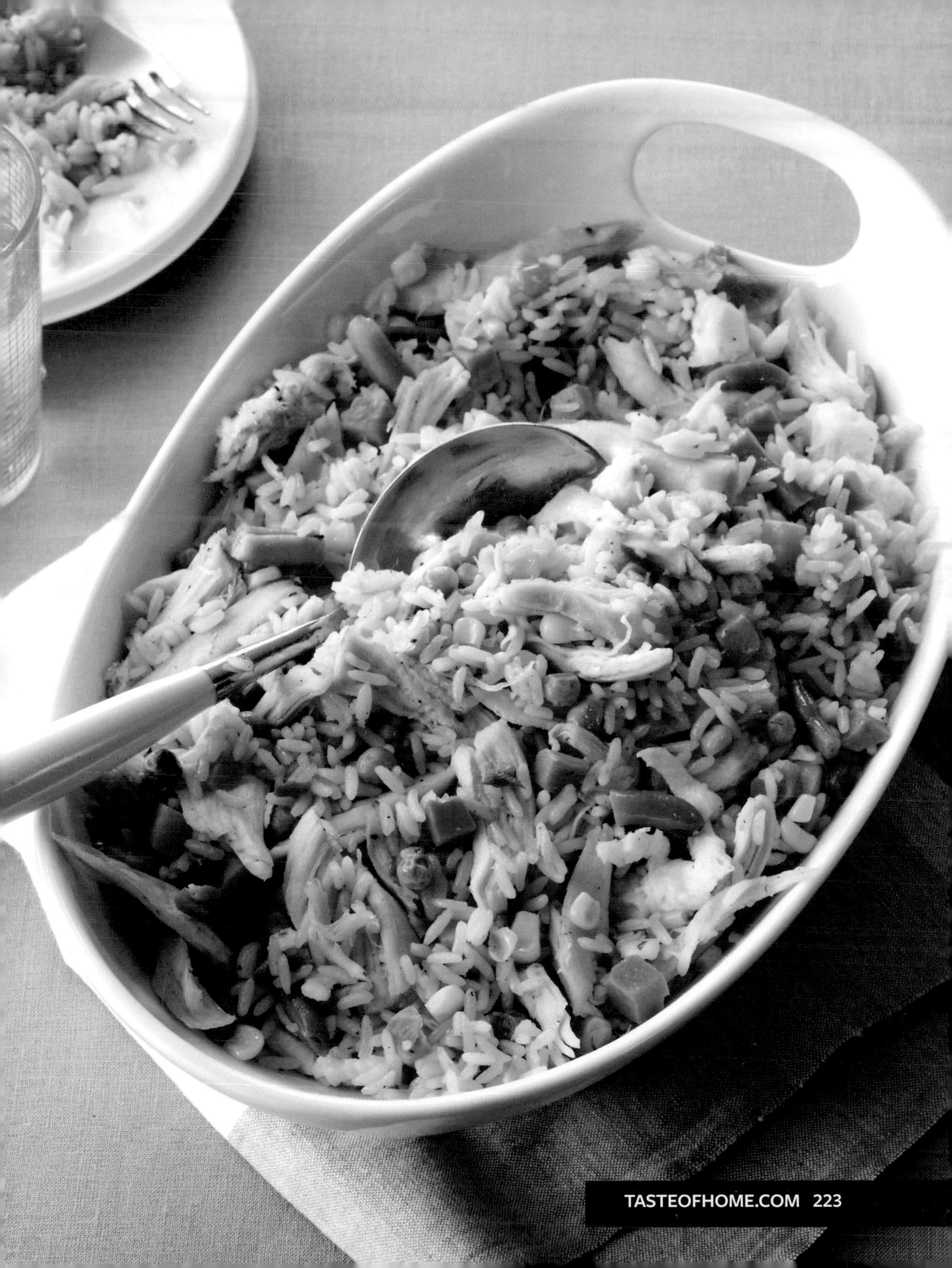

INSPIRED BY:
**MCDONALD'S
SHAMROCK SHAKE**

THIN MINT MILK SHAKE

Save a sleeve of those yummy chocolate-mint Girl Scout cookies to use for creamy milk shakes. They go over big with kids and adults alike.
—Shauna Sever, San Francisco, CA

Takes: 5 min. • **Makes:** 2 servings

- 3 Tbsp. creme de menthe or 3 Tbsp. 2% milk plus a dash of peppermint extract
- 1¼ to 1½ cups vanilla ice cream
- 7 Girl Scout Thin Mint cookies Green food coloring, optional

Place all ingredients in a blender in order listed; cover and process until blended. Serve immediately.

⅔ CUP: 363 cal., 12g fat (7g sat. fat), 36mg chol., 70mg sod., 49g carb. (47g sugars, 1g fiber), 3g pro.

CINNAMON SPICED APPLES

My cinnamon spiced apples are homey and aromatic. They're heavenly with a scoop of vanilla ice cream.

—Amie Powell, Knoxville, TN

Prep: 15 min. • **Cook:** 3 hours • **Makes:** 6 cups

⅓ cup sugar
¼ cup packed brown sugar
1 Tbsp. cornstarch
3 tsp. ground cinnamon
⅛ tsp. ground nutmeg
6 large Granny Smith apples, peeled and cut into eighths
¼ cup butter, cubed

In a small bowl, mix the first 5 ingredients. Place apples in a greased 5-qt. slow cooker; add sugar mixture and toss to coat. Top with butter. Cook, covered, on low 3-4 hours or until apples are tender, stirring halfway through cooking.

¾ CUP: 181 cal., 6g fat (4g sat. fat), 15mg chol., 48mg sod., 34g carb. (29g sugars, 2g fiber), 0 pro.

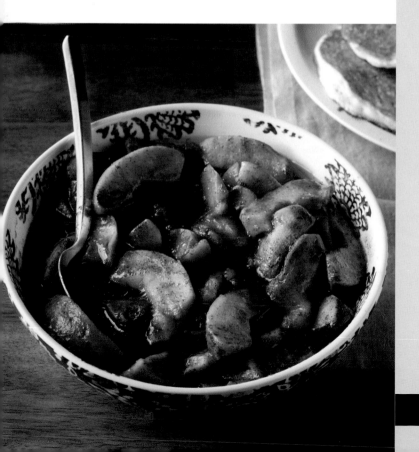

Double-Take Desserts

IS DESSERT THE BEST PART OF DINNER? IT JUST MIGHT BE! NOW YOU CAN HAVE ALL THE PLEASURES OF YOUR FAVORITE INDULGENT RESTAURANT TREATS WITHOUT LEAVING HOME.

KEY LIME PIE, P. 246
INSPIRED BY:
CALIFORNIA PIZZA KITCHEN'S
KEY LIME PIE

OLD-TIME CUSTARD ICE CREAM

My most memorable summertime dessert for get-togethers has always been homemade ice cream. This vanilla custard is so rich and creamy and the perfect splurge on a hot afternoon.
—Martha Self, Montgomery, TX

PREP: 55 min. + chilling • **PROCESS:** 55 min./batch + freezing
MAKES: 2¾ qt.

- 1½ **cups sugar**
- ¼ **cup all-purpose flour**
- ½ **tsp. salt**
- 4 **cups whole milk**
- 4 **large eggs, lightly beaten**
- 2 **pints heavy whipping cream**
- 3 **Tbsp. vanilla extract**

1. In a large heavy saucepan, combine sugar, flour and salt. Gradually add milk until smooth. Cook and stir over medium heat until thickened and bubbly. Reduce heat to low; cook and stir 2 minutes longer. Remove from heat.

2. In a small bowl, whisk a small amount of hot mixture into eggs; return all to pan, whisking constantly. Bring to a gentle boil; cook and stir 2 minutes. Remove from heat immediately.

3. Quickly transfer to a large bowl; place bowl in a pan of ice water. Stir gently and occasionally for 2 minutes. Press plastic wrap onto surface of custard. Refrigerate for several hours or overnight.

4. Stir cream and vanilla into custard. Fill cylinder of ice cream freezer two-thirds full; freeze according to manufacturer's directions. (Refrigerate remaining mixture until ready to freeze.) Transfer ice cream to freezer containers, allowing headspace for expansion. Freeze 2-4 hours or until firm. Repeat with remaining ice cream mixture.

½ CUP: 252 cal., 18g fat (11g sat. fat), 88mg chol., 98mg sod., 18g carb. (17g sugars, 0 fiber), 4g pro.

INSPIRED BY:
CULVER'S
VANILLA FROZEN CUSTARD

PEANUT BUTTER CUP CHEESECAKE

I brought this dessert to a holiday party. I'm sure you'll agree it tastes as luscious as it looks.

—Dawn Lowenstein, Huntingdon Valley, PA

PREP: 20 min. • **BAKE:** 55 min. + chilling • **MAKES:** 14 servings

- 1¼ cups graham cracker crumbs
- ¼ cup sugar
- ¼ cup Oreo cookie crumbs
- 6 Tbsp. butter, melted
- ¾ cup creamy peanut butter

FILLING

- 3 pkg. (8 oz. each) cream cheese, softened
- 1 cup sugar
- 1 cup sour cream
- 1½ tsp. vanilla extract
- 3 large eggs, room temperature, lightly beaten
- 1 cup hot fudge ice cream topping, divided
- 6 peanut butter cups, cut into small wedges

1. In a large bowl, combine the cracker crumbs, sugar, cookie crumbs and butter. Press onto the bottom and 1 in. up the sides of a greased 9-in. springform pan. Place on a baking sheet.

2. Bake at 350° for 7-9 minutes or until set. Cool on a wire rack. In a microwave-safe bowl, heat peanut butter on high for 30 seconds or until softened. Spread over crust to within 1 in. of edges.

3. In a large bowl, beat cream cheese and sugar until smooth. Beat in sour cream and vanilla. Add eggs; beat on low speed just until combined. Pour 1 cup of the filling into a bowl; set aside. Pour remaining filling over peanut butter layer.

4. In a microwave, heat ¼ cup fudge topping on high for 30 seconds or until thin; fold into reserved cream cheese mixture. Carefully pour over filling; cut through with a knife to swirl.

5. Return pan to baking sheet. Bake at 350° for 55-65 minutes or until center is almost set. Cool on a wire rack for 10 minutes. Carefully run a knife around edge of pan to loosen; cool 1 hour longer.

6. Microwave remaining fudge topping for 30 seconds or until warmed; spread over cheesecake. Garnish with peanut butter cups. Refrigerate overnight. Refrigerate leftovers.

NOTE: Reduced-fat peanut butter is not recommended for this recipe.

1 SLICE: 574 cal., 39g fat (18g sat. fat), 106mg chol., 380mg sod., 50g carb. (38g sugars, 2g fiber), 11g pro.

INSPIRED BY:
COUNTRY KITCHEN'S
OLD FASHIONED APPLE CRISP

WINNING APPLE CRISP

I live in apple country, and making a delicious apple crisp is one way to use them up. And it doesn't take a lot of time to assemble.
—Gertrude Bartnick, Portage, WI

PREP: 20 min. • **BAKE:** 1 hour • **MAKES:** 8 servings

- 1   cup all-purpose flour
- ¾   cup rolled oats
- 1   cup packed brown sugar
- 1   tsp. ground cinnamon
- ½   cup butter, softened
- 4   cups chopped peeled apples
- 1   cup sugar
- 2   Tbsp. cornstarch
- 1   cup water
- 1   tsp. vanilla extract
      Vanilla ice cream, optional

1. Preheat oven to 350°. In a large bowl, combine the first 4 ingredients. Cut in butter until crumbly. Press half into a greased 2½-qt. baking dish or a 9-in. square baking pan. Cover with apples.
2. In a small saucepan, combine the sugar, cornstarch, water and vanilla. Bring to a boil; cook and stir 2 minutes or until thick and clear. Pour over apples. Sprinkle with remaining crumb mixture.
3. Bake 60-65 minutes or until apples are tender. Serve warm, with ice cream if desired.
1 SERVING: 426 cal., 12g fat (7g sat. fat), 31mg chol., 127mg sod., 79g carb. (58g sugars, 2g fiber), 3g pro.

BEST EVER CHEESECAKE

I've passed this recipe to dozens of folks. My daughter is so fond of this classic cheesecake she served it at her wedding instead of traditional cake.

—Howard Koch, Lima, OH

PREP: 20 min. + chilling • **BAKE:** 35 min. + chilling • **MAKES:** 8 servings

- 1¼ cups graham cracker crumbs
- ⅓ cup butter, melted
- ¼ cup sugar

FILLING/TOPPING
- 2 pkg. (8 oz. each) cream cheese, softened
- 2 large eggs, room temperature, lightly beaten
- ⅔ cup sugar, divided
- 2 tsp. vanilla extract, divided
  Pinch of salt
- 1 cup sour cream

1. In a bowl, combine the graham cracker crumbs, butter and sugar. Pat onto the bottom and up the sides of a 9-in. pie plate. Chill.

2. For filling, beat cream cheese and eggs in a bowl on medium speed for 1 minute. Add ⅓ cup sugar, 1 tsp. vanilla and salt. Continue beating until well blended, about 1 minute. Pour into crust.

3. Bake at 350° for 35 minutes. Cool for 10 minutes. For topping, combine the sour cream and remaining sugar and vanilla in a small bowl; spread over cheesecake. Bake for 10 minutes. Cool completely on a wire rack. Refrigerate 3 hours or overnight.

1 PIECE: 388 cal., 25g fat (15g sat. fat), 124mg chol., 289mg sod., 35g carb. (26g sugars, 0 fiber), 6g pro.

RAWHIDE WHISKEY CAKE

For several years, our neighbor gave us a moist, whiskey-flavored cake around the holidays. I've tweaked the recipe, and now my friends want this cake instead of homemade cookie platters.
—Cindy Worth, Lapwai, ID

PREP: 15 min. + standing • **BAKE:** 1 hour + cooling
MAKES: 16 slices

- 1 pkg. spice cake mix with pudding (regular size)
- 1 pkg. (3.4 oz.) instant vanilla pudding mix
- ¾ cup 2% milk
- ¾ cup whiskey
- ½ cup canola oil
- 4 large eggs, room temperature
- 1⅓ cups coarsely chopped walnuts, divided

GLAZE
- 1 cup sugar
- ½ cup butter, cubed
- ½ cup whiskey
- 1 tsp. water

1. Preheat oven to 300°. Grease and flour a 10-in. tube pan.
2. Combine the first 6 ingredients; beat on low speed 30 seconds. Beat on medium speed 2 minutes; fold in 1 cup nuts. Pour batter into prepared pan; sprinkle with remaining nuts. Bake until a toothpick inserted in center comes out clean, 60-65 minutes. Cool in pan.
3. For glaze, mix all ingredients in a small saucepan; bring to a boil over medium-high heat. Reduce heat; simmer 10 minutes. Cool 3 minutes. Pour one-third of glaze over top of cake, allowing some to flow over sides. Let stand 1 hour. Remove from pan to cool completely; cover.
4. The next day, reheat glaze; brush half over cake, cooling before covering. Repeat the following day, using remaining glaze.

1 SLICE: 400 cal., 23g fat (6g sat. fat), 63mg chol., 298mg sod., 43g carb. (30g sugars, 1g fiber), 5g pro.

HAVE IT YOUR WAY
This cake requires planning ahead. You'll need three days from mixing to ta-da! To make sure your cake pops out perfectly, use solid shortening to grease the cake pan. Also be sure to splurge on a good whiskey. Buy a pint for the perfect amount.

VANILLA BEAN CUPCAKES

My young son is crazy for these cupcakes. Flecks of vanilla bean in the moist, tender cake and fancy decorations on top give them special-occasion status. But don't wait for a party to enjoy them!
—Alysha Braun, St. Catharines, ON

PREP: 30 min. • **BAKE:** 20 min. + cooling • **MAKES:** 1½ dozen

  ¾ cup unsalted butter, softened
1¼ cups sugar
  2 large eggs, room temperature
  2 vanilla beans
  2 cups cake flour
  2 tsp. baking powder
  ½ tsp. salt
  ⅔ cup whole milk
FROSTING
  1 pkg. (8 oz.) cream cheese, softened
  6 Tbsp. unsalted butter, softened
1½ tsp. vanilla extract
  3 cups confectioners' sugar
     Assorted candies and coarse sugar

1. Preheat oven to 375°. Line 18 muffin cups with paper liners.
2. In a large bowl, cream butter and sugar until light and fluffy. Add eggs, one at a time, beating well after each addition. Split vanilla beans lengthwise; using the tip of a sharp knife, scrape seeds from the center into creamed mixture. In another bowl, whisk flour, baking powder and salt; add to creamed mixture alternately with milk, beating well after each addition.
3. Fill prepared cups three-fourths full. Bake 16-18 minutes or until a toothpick inserted in center comes out clean. Cool in pans 10 minutes before removing to wire racks to cool completely.
4. In a large bowl, beat cream cheese, butter and vanilla until blended. Gradually beat in confectioners' sugar until smooth. Frost cupcakes. Decorate with candies and coarse sugar as desired. Refrigerate leftovers.
FREEZE OPTION: Freeze cooled cupcakes in freezer containers. To use, thaw at room temperature. Frost as directed.
1 CUPCAKE: 266 cal., 13g fat (8g sat. fat), 56mg chol., 143mg sod., 36g carb. (24g sugars, 0 fiber), 3g pro.

OLD-FASHIONED CUSTARD PIE

This recipe came from the best cook in West Virginia—my mother! I just added a little to her ingredients. I make my custard pie mostly for church and club functions. It's wonderfully different from all the other pies in my recipe collection.

—Maxine Linkenauger, Montverde, FL

PREP: 20 min. + chilling • **BAKE:** 25 min. + chilling
MAKES: 8 servings

Pastry for single-crust pie (9 in.)
- 4 large eggs, room temperature
- 2½ cups whole milk
- ½ cup sugar
- 1 tsp. ground nutmeg
- 1 tsp. vanilla extract
- 1 tsp. almond extract
- ½ tsp. salt

1. Unroll crust into a 9-in. pie plate; flute edge. Refrigerate for 30 minutes. Preheat oven to 400°.

2. Line unpricked crust with a double thickness of foil. Fill with pie weights, dried beans or uncooked rice. Bake on a lower oven rack until edges are golden brown, 10-15 minutes. Remove foil and weights; bake until bottom is golden brown, 3-6 minutes longer. Cool on a wire rack.

3. In a large bowl, whisk eggs. Whisk in remaining ingredients until blended. Pour into crust. Cover edges with foil. Bake at 400° until a knife inserted in the center comes out clean, 25-30 minutes. Cool on a wire rack for 1 hour. Refrigerate for at least 3 hours before serving. Refrigerate leftovers.

1 PIECE: 258 cal., 12g fat (5g sat. fat), 122mg chol., 317mg sod., 30g carb. (17g sugars, 0 fiber), 7g pro.

INSPIRED BY:
BAKERS SQUARE'S CUSTARD PIE

INSPIRED BY:
OLIVE GARDEN'S
TIRAMISU

MAKE-AHEAD TIRAMISU

My variation of the popular Italian dessert is so easy to assemble. It's convenient, too, because you can make it the day before your dinner party or potluck.
—Linda Finn, Louisville, MS

PREP: 25 min. + chilling • **MAKES:** 12 servings

½	cup strong brewed coffee
2	Tbsp. coffee liqueur
16	oz. cream cheese, softened
⅔	cup sugar
2	cups sour cream
¼	cup 2% milk
½	tsp. vanilla extract
2	pkg. (3 oz. each) ladyfingers, split
1	Tbsp. baking cocoa

1. In a small bowl, combine coffee and liqueur; set aside.

2. In a large bowl, beat cream cheese and sugar until smooth. Beat in sour cream, milk and vanilla until blended.

3. Layer 1 package of ladyfingers in an ungreased 11x7-in. dish; brush with half of coffee mixture. Top with half of cream cheese mixture. Repeat layers (dish will be full).

4. Cover and refrigerate 8 hours or overnight. Just before serving, sprinkle with cocoa.

1 PIECE: 321 cal., 21g fat (14g sat. fat), 100mg chol., 149mg sod., 24g carb. (14g sugars, 0 fiber), 6g pro.

WHITE CHOCOLATE PEPPERMINT CRUNCH

Here's my favorite minty confection to make at Christmas. It's easy and delicious. I fill small bags with the crunchy candy and place them in gift baskets.
—Nancy Shelton, Boaz, KY

PREP: 15 min. + chilling • **COOK:** 5 min. • **MAKES:** about 1½ lbs.

- 1 lb. white candy coating, coarsely chopped
- 1 Tbsp. butter
- 1 Tbsp. canola oil
- 1 cup chopped peppermint candies or candy canes

1. Line a baking sheet with parchment or waxed paper. In a microwave, melt candy coating; stir until smooth. Stir in butter and oil until blended. Stir in candies. Spread to desired thickness on prepared pan.

2. Refrigerate until firm. Break into pieces. Store in an airtight container in the refrigerator.

1 OZ.: 125 cal., 6g fat (5g sat. fat), 1mg chol., 5mg sod., 17g carb. (15g sugars, 0 fiber), 0 pro.

INSPIRED BY:
GHIRARDELLI CHOCOLATE COMPANY'S PEPPERMINT BARK

WALNUT STREUSEL COFFEE CAKE

I love this cake from my Aunt Suzie, especially the nice moist texture and sweet surprise of the brown sugar-nut mixture inside. It's great with a cup of coffee.

—Michelle Eder, Grand Rapids, MI

PREP: 20 min. • **BAKE:** 45 min. + cooling • **MAKES:** 12 servings

- 1 cup chopped walnuts
- ½ cup packed brown sugar
- 2 Tbsp. butter, melted
- ½ tsp. ground cinnamon

COFFEE CAKE

- 4 large eggs, separated
- 1 cup butter, softened
- 1¾ cups sugar
- 1 tsp. vanilla extract
- 3 cups all-purpose flour
- 2 tsp. baking powder
- ½ tsp. baking soda
- ¼ tsp. salt
- 1 cup sour cream
- 2 tsp. confectioners' sugar

1. In a small bowl, mix walnuts, brown sugar, butter and cinnamon. Place egg whites in a large bowl; let stand at room temperature 30 minutes. Preheat oven to 350°. Grease and flour a 10-in. fluted tube pan.

2. In a large bowl, cream butter and sugar until light and fluffy. Gradually add egg yolks. Beat in vanilla. In another bowl, whisk flour, baking powder, baking soda and salt; add to creamed mixture alternately with sour cream, beating well after each addition.

3. With clean beaters, beat egg whites on medium speed until stiff peaks form. Fold into batter.

4. Pour half of the batter into prepared pan; sprinkle with walnut mixture. Pour in remaining batter. Bake 45-55 minutes or until a toothpick inserted in center comes out clean. Cool 10 minutes before removing from pan to a wire rack to cool completely. Dust with confectioners' sugar.

NOTE: For easier removal of cakes, use solid shortening to grease plain and fluted tube pans.

1 SLICE: 540 cal., 29g fat (14g sat. fat), 128mg chol., 323mg sod., 65g carb. (40g sugars, 2g fiber), 8g pro.

NICE & SOFT SUGAR COOKIES

My family's all-time favorite Christmas cookie has had a million different shapes over the years. Little ones have fun choosing their own designs.
—Cathy Hall, Lyndhurst, VA

PREP: 45 min. + chilling • **BAKE:** 5 min./batch + cooling
MAKES: about 3 dozen

- 1 **cup butter, softened**
- 1½ **cups confectioners' sugar**
- 1 **large egg, room temperature**
- 1½ **tsp. vanilla extract**
- 2½ **cups self-rising flour**

ICING

- 2½ **cups confectioners' sugar**
- ¼ **cup water**
- 4 **tsp. meringue powder**
- ¼ **cup light corn syrup**
  Food coloring of choice
  Colored sugar and sprinkles, optional

1. Cream butter and confectioners' sugar until light and fluffy, beat in egg and vanilla. Gradually beat in flour. Divide dough in half. Wrap each in plastic; refrigerate 2 hours or until dough is firm enough to roll.

2. Preheat oven to 375°. On a floured surface, roll each portion of dough to ³⁄₁₆-in. thickness. Cut with floured 3-in. cookie cutters. Place 2 in. apart on ungreased baking sheets. Bake until set, 5-7 minutes. Cool on pans 2 minutes; remove to wire racks to cool completely.

3. Beat confectioners' sugar, water and meringue powder on low speed until blended; beat on high until soft peaks form, about 4 minutes. Add corn syrup; beat 1 minute.

4. Tint with food coloring as desired. (Always keep unused icing covered with a damp cloth; if necessary, beat again on high speed to restore texture.) Pipe or spread icing on cookies; decorate as desired. Let dry.

NOTE: As a substitute for 2½ cups of self-rising flour, place 3¾ tsp. baking powder and 1¼ tsp. salt in a 1-cup measuring cup. Add all-purpose flour to measure 1 cup; combine with an additional 1½ cups all-purpose flour.

1 COOKIE: 138 cal., 5g fat (3g sat. fat), 19mg chol., 150mg sod., 22g carb. (15g sugars, 0 fiber), 1g pro.

HAVE IT YOUR WAY

Here's an easy way to add sparkle to sugar cookies. While they're still warm, brush each cookie lightly with corn syrup and sprinkle with your favorite flavor of gelatin right from the package.

KEY LIME PIE

We created this refreshing pie with a homemade crumb crust and a creamy lime filling to bring a little bit of the tropics to the North. If you can't find Key lime juice, regular lime juice works fine, too.
—*Taste of Home* Test Kitchen

PREP: 30 min. + chilling • **MAKES:** 4 servings

⅔ cup graham cracker crumbs
2 Tbsp. sugar
3 Tbsp. butter, melted
FILLING
½ cup sugar
2 Tbsp. all-purpose flour
1 Tbsp. plus 1½ tsp. cornstarch
⅛ tsp. salt
1 cup water
1 drop green food coloring, optional
2 large egg yolks, beaten
2 Tbsp. Key lime juice
1 tsp. butter
½ tsp. grated lime zest
Whipped cream, optional
Thinly sliced Key limes and additional grated lime zest, optional

1. In a small bowl, combine cracker crumbs and sugar; stir in butter. Press onto the bottom and up the sides of a 7-in. pie plate coated with cooking spray. Bake at 325° for 8-10 minutes or until lightly browned. Cool on a wire rack.
2. In a small saucepan, combine the sugar, flour, cornstarch and salt; gradually stir in water and food coloring if desired. Cook and stir over medium heat until thickened. Remove from the heat. Stir a small amount of hot filling into egg yolks; return all to the pan, stirring constantly. Bring to a gentle boil; cook and stir 2 minutes longer. Remove from the heat. Gently stir in lime juice, butter and lime zest.
3. Pour into crust. Cool for 15 minutes. Refrigerate for 1-2 hours. Garnish with whipped cream, lime slices and zest if desired. Refrigerate leftovers.
1 PIECE: 321 cal., 13g fat (7g sat. fat), 132mg chol., 259mg sod., 49g carb. (33g sugars, 1g fiber), 3g pro.

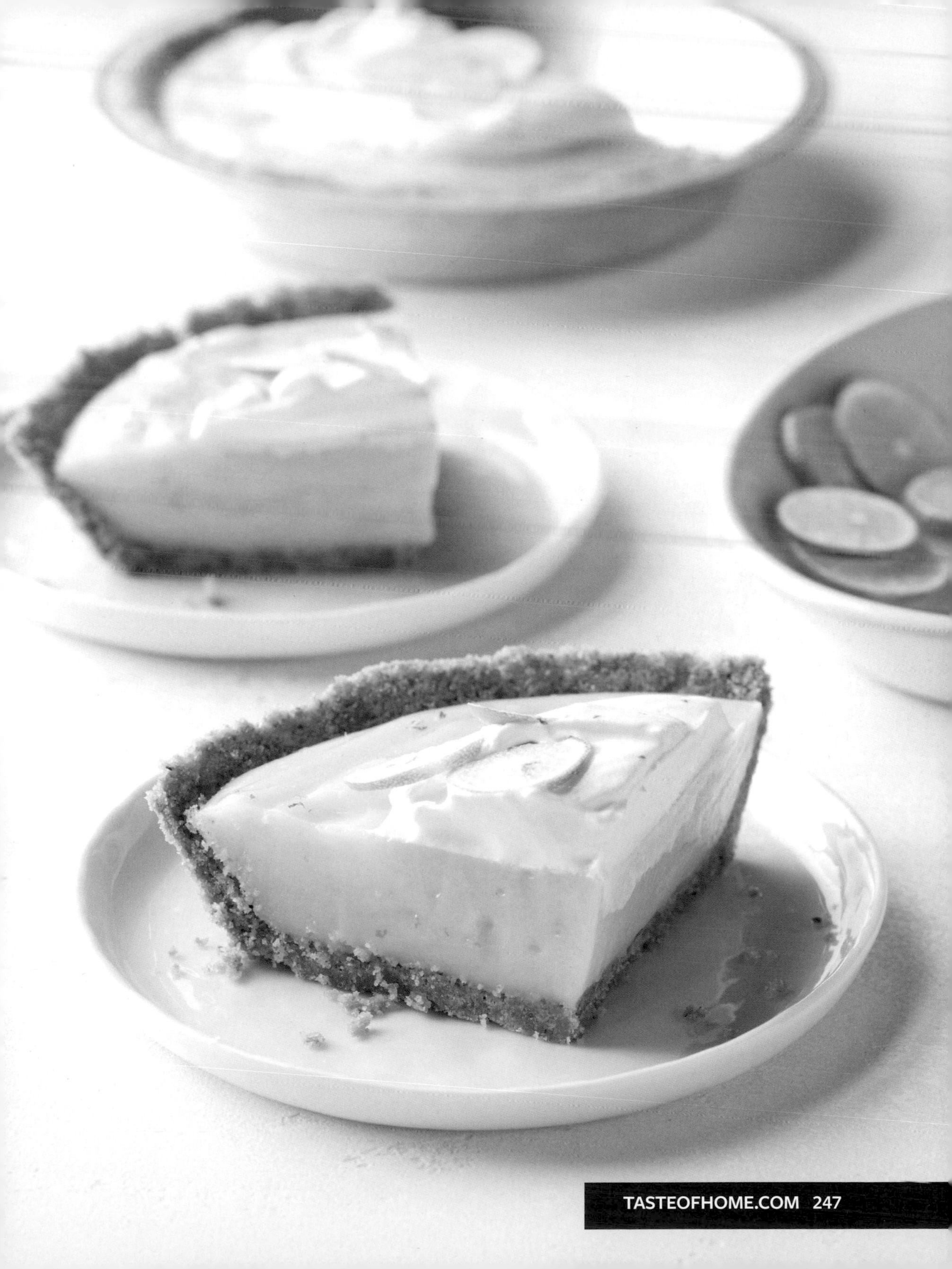

BLOND BROWNIES A LA MODE

We have a lot of church socials so I'm always looking for something new and different to bring. Drizzled with a sweet maple sauce, these brownies are wonderful with or without the ice cream.
—Ollie Parker, Chester, SC

INSPIRED BY:
APPLEBEE'S
MAPLE BUTTER BLONDIE

PREP: 25 min. • **BAKE:** 25 min. + cooling • **MAKES:** 20 servings

- ¾ cup butter, softened
- 2 cups packed brown sugar
- 4 large eggs, room temperature
- 2 tsp. vanilla extract
- 2 cups all-purpose flour
- 2 tsp. baking powder
- 1 tsp. salt
- 1½ cups chopped pecans

MAPLE CREAM SAUCE
- 1 cup maple syrup
- 2 Tbsp. butter
- ¼ cup evaporated milk
  Vanilla ice cream and chopped pecans

1. In a large bowl, cream butter and brown sugar until light and fluffy. Beat in eggs and vanilla. Combine the flour, baking powder and salt; gradually add to creamed mixture. Stir in pecans.
2. Spread into a greased 13x9-in. baking pan. Bake at 350° for 25-30 minutes or until a toothpick inserted in the center comes out clean. Cool on a wire rack.
3. For the sauce, combine syrup and butter in a saucepan. Bring to a boil; cook and stir for 3 minutes. Remove from the heat; stir in milk. Cut brownies into squares; cut in half if desired.
4. Place on dessert plates with a scoop of ice cream. Top with sauce; sprinkle with pecans.

1 SERVING: 322 cal., 16g fat (6g sat. fat), 65mg chol., 265mg sod., 43g carb. (33g sugars, 1g fiber), 4g pro.

INSPIRED BY:
PORTILLO'S
FAMOUS CHOCOLATE CAKE

CLASSIC CHOCOLATE CAKE

This recipe appeared on a can of Hershey's Cocoa way back in 1943. I made it, my boys liked it and I've been making it ever since. I make all my cakes from scratch, and this is one of the best!
—Betty Follas, Morgan Hill, CA

PREP: 15 min. • **BAKE:** 35 min. • **MAKES:** 15 servings

- ⅔ cup butter, softened
- 1⅔ cups sugar
- 3 large eggs, room temperature
- 2 cups all-purpose flour
- ⅔ cup baking cocoa
- 1¼ tsp. baking soda
- 1 tsp. salt
- 1⅓ cups whole milk
  Confectioners' sugar or favorite frosting

1. In a bowl, cream butter and sugar until fluffy. Add eggs, one at a time, beating well after each addition. Combine flour, cocoa, baking soda and salt; add to creamed mixture alternately with milk, beating until smooth after each addition. Pour batter into a greased and floured 13x9-in. pan.
2. Bake at 350° until a toothpick inserted in center comes out clean, 35-40 minutes. Cool on a wire rack. When cake is cool, dust with confectioners' sugar or frost with your favorite frosting.
1 PIECE: 257 cal., 10g fat (6g sat. fat), 67mg chol., 368mg sod., 38g carb. (23g sugars, 1g fiber), 4g pro.

STRAWBERRY SHORTCAKE CUPS

My grandmother passed this recipe down to my mother. They both remembered the days when store-bought shortcake was unheard of. Mother later shared it with me, and I've since given it to my daughter.
—Althea Heers, Jewell, IA

Prep: 15 min. • **Bake:** 15 min. + cooling • **Makes:** 8 servings

- 1 qt. fresh strawberries
- 4 Tbsp. sugar, divided
- 1½ cups all-purpose flour
- 1 Tbsp. baking powder
- ½ tsp. salt
- ¼ cup cold butter, cubed
- 1 large egg, room temperature
- ½ cup whole milk
  Whipped cream

1. Mash or slice the strawberries; place in a large bowl. Add 2 Tbsp. sugar and set aside. In another bowl, combine flour, baking powder, salt and remaining sugar; cut in butter until crumbly. In a small bowl, beat egg and milk; stir into flour mixture just until moistened.
2. Fill 8 greased muffin cups two-thirds full. Bake at 425° until golden, about 12 minutes. Remove from pan to cool on a wire rack.
3. Just before serving, split shortcakes in half horizontally. Spoon the strawberries and whipped cream between layers and over tops of shortcakes.
1 SERVING: 200 cal., 7g fat (4g sat. fat), 44mg chol., 372mg sod., 30g carb. (11g sugars, 2g fiber), 4g pro.

CARROT CAKE WITH PECAN FROSTING

This impressive cake is one of my husband's favorites. It's homey and old-fashioned—perfect for holidays or Sunday family dinners.
—Adrian Badon, Denham Springs, LA

PREP: 35 min. • **BAKE:** 40 min. + cooling • **MAKES:** 16 servings

- 1 cup shortening
- 2 cups sugar
- 4 large eggs, room temperature
- 1 can (8 oz.) unsweetened crushed pineapple, undrained
- 2½ cups all-purpose flour
- 2 tsp. ground cinnamon
- 1 tsp. baking powder
- 1 tsp. baking soda
- ¾ tsp. salt
- 3 cups shredded carrots (about 6 medium carrots)

FROSTING
- 1 pkg. (8 oz.) reduced-fat cream cheese
- ½ cup butter, softened
- 1 tsp. vanilla extract
- 3¾ cups confectioners' sugar
- 1 cup chopped pecans

1. Preheat oven to 325°. Line bottoms of 2 greased 9-in. round baking pans with parchment; grease paper.

2. In a large bowl, cream shortening and sugar until fluffy. Add eggs, 1 at a time, beating well after each addition. Beat in pineapple. In another bowl, whisk flour, cinnamon, baking powder, baking soda and salt; gradually add to creamed mixture. Stir in carrots.

3. Transfer batter to prepared pans. Bake until a toothpick inserted in center comes out clean, 40-45 minutes. Cool in pans 10 minutes before removing to wire racks; remove paper. Cool completely.

4. In a large bowl, beat cream cheese, butter and vanilla until blended. Gradually beat in confectioners' sugar until smooth. Stir in pecans.

5. Spread frosting between layers and over top and sides of cake. Refrigerate until serving.

1 SLICE: 557 cal., 27g fat (10g sat. fat), 72mg chol., 358mg sod., 74g carb. (57g sugars, 2g fiber), 6g pro.

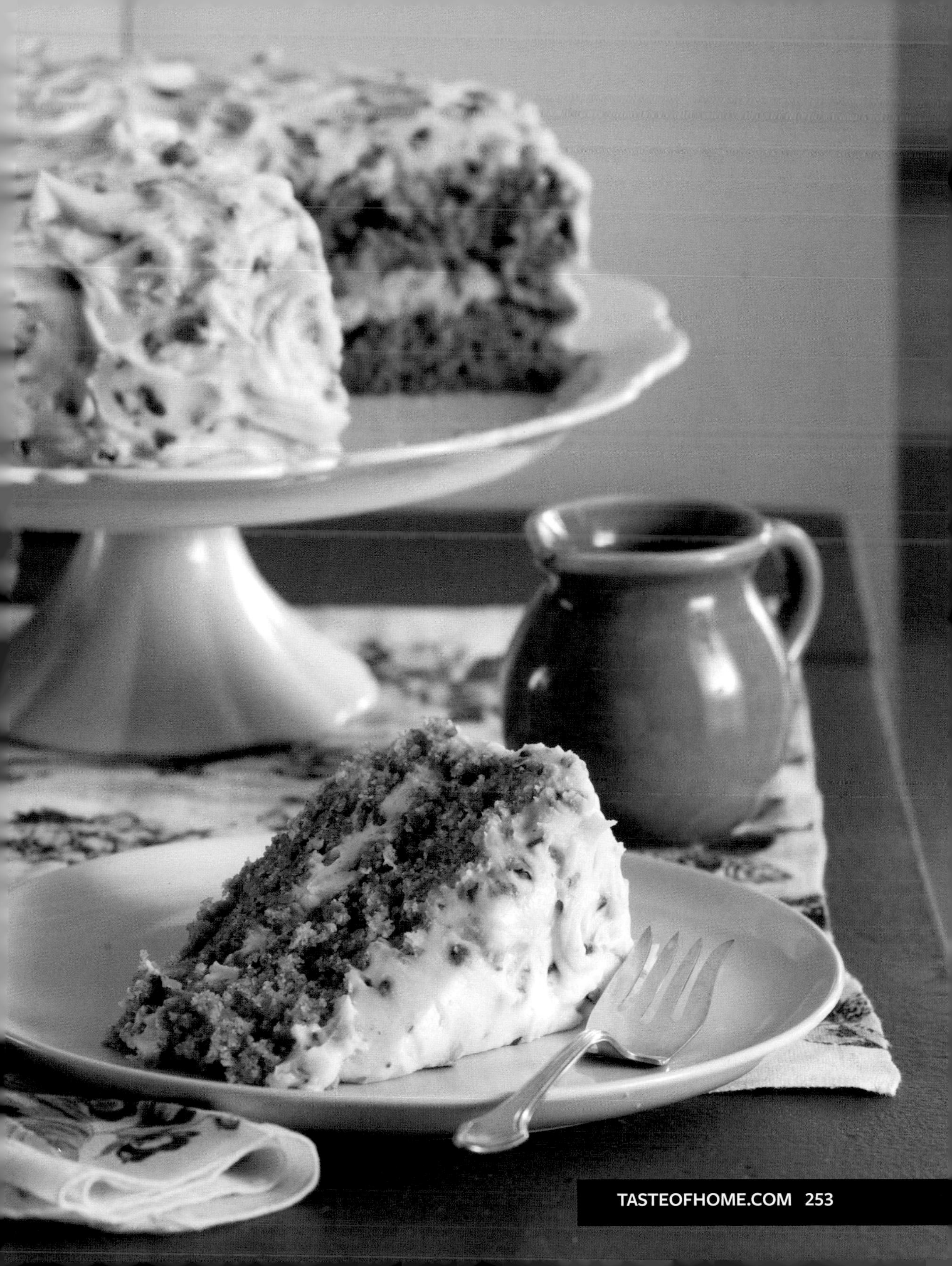

Recipe Index